THE
GREAT
AMERICAN
CONVERTIBLE

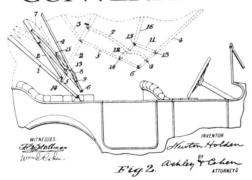

Somewhere West of Laramie

SOMEWHERE west of Laramie there's a broncho-busting, steer-roping girl who knows what I'm talking about.

She can tell what a sassy pony, that's a cross between greased lightning and the place where it hits, can do with eleven hundred pounds of steel and action when he's going high, wide and handsome.

The truth is—the Playboy was built for her.

Built for the lass whose face is brown with the sun when the day is done of revel and romp and race.

She loves the cross of the wild and the tame.

There's a savor of links about that car—of laughter and lilt and light—a hint of old loves—and saddle and quirt. It's a brawny thing—yet a graceful thing for the sweep o' the Avenue.

Step into the Playboy when the hour grows dull with things gone dead and stale.

Then start for the land of real living with the spirit of the lass who rides, lean and rangy, into the red horizon of a Wyoming twilight.

JORDAN
JORDAN MOTOR CAR COMPANY, Inc., Cleveland, Ohio

THE GREAT AMERICAN CONVERTIBLE

AN AFFECTIONATE GUIDE

by Robert Wieder & George Hall

Designed by Dugald Stermer

⟦*Doubleday / Dolphin*⟧

Doubleday & Company, Inc.

Garden City, New York
1977

Photo credits:

Pp. 24, 26, 28, courtesy of Culver Pictures, Inc; p. 30, courtesy of the Elton Hunt Collection; p. 32, courtesy of the Donald J. Narus Collection; p. 35, courtesy of the American Motors Corporation; p. 38, courtesy of the Buick Motor Division; p. 116, courtesy of Nudie's Rodeo Tailors; p. 120, courtesy of *Autoweek* magazine; p. 128, courtesy of the Donald J. Narus Collection; p. 129, courtesy of the Ford Motor Company; p. 140, courtesy of the Donald J. Narus Collection.

THE GREAT AMERICAN CONVERTIBLE
was produced and directed by
Baron Wolman/Squarebooks,
Post Office Box 144, Mill Valley, California 94941

Text copyright ©1977 by Robert Wieder
Photographs copyright ©1977 by George Hall

Library of Congress Catalog Card Number: 77-72416
ISBN: 0-385-13123-2

[INTRODUCTION:]

WHEN WE WERE FIRST APPROACHED with the idea of producing a book about the American convertible, our reaction was classically skeptical. We assumed there were at least several books on the subject already floating around libraries and specialty bookstores. After all, few institutions have produced more literature than the automobile. And for a fourth of its life, the car was overwhelmingly a retractable-top item. Of the 8,000,000 American autos built through 1920, for example, the vast majority had cloth tops. There are books on sports cars, steam cars, race cars, antique cars, vans, trucks, station wagons, fire engines and hotrods. Surely there had to be a definitive volume on the life, death and significance of the vehicle which for 30 years was our major form of transportation—the collapsing-top car.

But if such a book existed, we had no luck finding it, no more than we had finding magazines or car clubs organized around the "ragtop." Auto buffs—the most club-forming group this side of war vets—have organizations honoring antiques, sports cars, trucks, woodies, vans, Fords, Buicks, indeed everything from Tuckers to Stutzes to Marmons; even clubs expressly for the owners of front-wheel drive Cadillacs and curved-dash Oldsmobiles. There were clubs for early T-Birds and Ford Retractables; but despite the fact that most convertible owners refer to themselves as "convertible people" and consider all other convertible drivers to be virtual brethren, there seems to be no national organization in simple celebration of the convertible.

At this point, we began to wonder if anyone out there *cared* about convertibles.

We didn't have to wonder long. The moment we let it be known that we were putting together a book on open cars, people and testimonials flew out of the woodwork. Convertible-freaks may lack organization, but not numbers. If we had a dollar for everyone who swore the greatest car of his/her life was an old ragtop, we could have skipped the book and simply retired.

Even amidst this torrential enthusiasm, there was still more published data about Bigfoot than about the open car, and our research quickly became a matter of endlessly gleaning specific open-car references from larger works, pouring through production records and automotive histories, and wringing information from owners and collectors. If we had one advantage going for us, it was our location: the convertible capital of the cosmos, California. As many as three-fourths of all surviving ragtops may be out here, as well as at least that proportion of collectors and connoisseurs.

Another advantage to our work was convertible-people themselves, who are anything but secretive and reticent, especially on the subject of their cars. Ragtop-lovers come in all sizes, ages, sexes and types, from mechanical wizards to automotive dunces, from retired Generals to career ladies. What they have in common is a sense of selectivity—of being a cut above the routine motoring cloth—and a willingness to talk you deaf on the virtues of the open car.

Even with all this verbal input, there will undoubtedly be something lacking in the book for everyone: a milestone unmentioned, a classic not included in the Catalog, a factor deleted from the Buyer's Checklist, etc. Not every salient fact, tip, photo and date could be hammered into the available space. But even with its inevitable flaws, presumptions and omissions, it is, at least and at last, a book about the life and times of the American convertible. We are glad we did it.

We're also glad that the world is full of people ever eager to offer suggestions, information, knowledge, experience, help and time to projects like this. Specifically, we owe great debts to Jim Ashworth, David Moe, Owen Owens, Ed and Charlie Goodman, Mary Tonon, Don Narus, Tom and Cynthia Walsh, Baron Wolman, Dave Granados, Danny Wheeler, and Ed Beaumont. Without them the first book on convertibles would still be a gleam in our lens. We thank them, and tip our hat to people like them everywhere, for whom the ragtop is a joy immortal. This is their book. It is dedicated to them and to the car whose top went down.

Long may they drive.

—George Hall
Bob Wieder

[TABLE OF CONTENTS]

1,305,185.

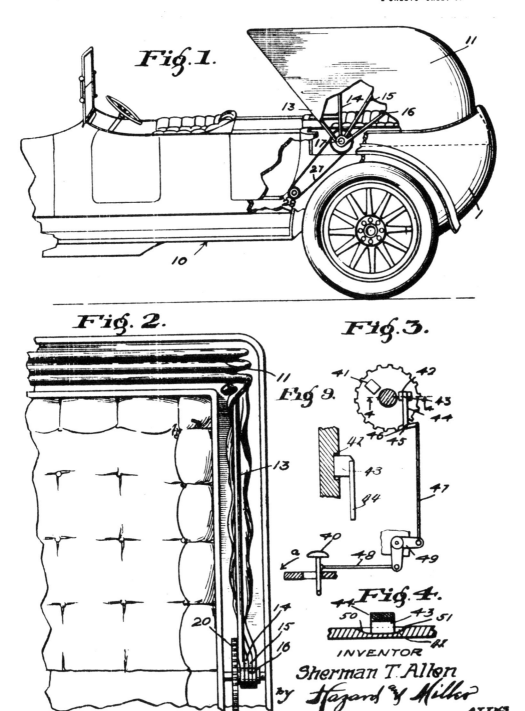

Fig. 1.

Fig. 2.

Fig. 3.

Fig. 9.

Fig. 4.

INVENTOR
Sherman T. Allen
By Hazard & Miller
ATT'YS

H. W. DE RUITER.
AUTOMOBILE TOP.
APPLICATION FILED JULY 27, 1916.

1,301,402.

Patented Apr. 22, 1919.

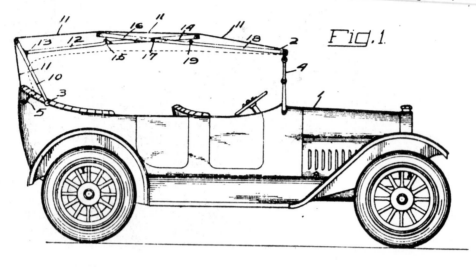

Fig. 1.

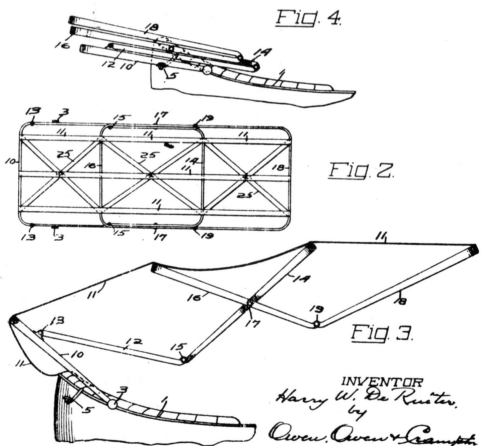

Fig. 4.

Fig. 2.

Fig. 3.

INVENTOR
Harry W. De Ruiter.
by
Owen, Owen & Crampton

[IN THE BEGINNING, THERE WAS LIGHT. AND WIND.

AND WEATHER...]

MOST OF THE CARS which made American automotive history had one thing in common: the absence of a hard top.

The first car patented had no top at all. Neither did the Stanley Steamer, the original "Merry Oldsmobile," or the flivver—Ford's first Tin Lizzie. The first transcontinental auto race in 1905 was won by a topless car, in 44 days. Some had tops of cloth: the 1893 Duryea "Motor Wagon," the first car produced by a moving assembly line (Ford, 1914), and the first Chevy. The 1928–32 Model A, perhaps the definitive American motorcar, had a fabric. So did most auto classics, from the Cord and Duesenberg to the T–Bird and Corvette. By 1930, hardtops would dominate the market, but cars with lowerable tops survived and were called by such colorful and affectionate names as "ragtops," "connies" and "clothtops." Anyone who ever had fun on the road, or even considered it a place for good times, had some memory or anecdote about driving with the top down. The convertible was a dazzling symbol of adventure, vigor and the good life for over half a century, synonymous with celebrity and elegance, with cruising and hotrodding.

Then came 1976, our 200th birthday, a year-long frenzy of the celebration, resurrection, preservation and evocative idolization of every imaginable bit of Americana. From cellophane to the Bill of Rights, every achievement that reflected a meaningful part of American history went into the time capsule, on display, or atop the pedestal. Except the ragtop, which went into extinction. 1976 was the last year in which any domestic auto company in America manufactured the convertible car; the Cadillac Motor Company—the last stand of many automotive extravagances—turned out its last non-hardtop El Dorado in April of that Bicentennial year.

You could say that on that April day something died in the American spirit—but only if you were a poet. The truth is that whatever the ragtop's unique spirit was, it had been dust for almost a decade. The story of how the convertible car went from universal popularity to oblivion in 60 years is a fascinating one, and it began—and ended—with us, the American motoring public, and how we viewed driving and ourselves.

Here's what happened:

HELP WANTED—MALE

THE FIRST CARS had no tops, period. The "horseless carriage" was no more than a buggy with a gas engine. In the 1900's there was no point to windows or a metal roof. Feeble early horsepowers couldn't work up a discomforting velocity anyway, and the weight of a hard top would surely have exhausted them; moreover, the added costs would have been intolerable. At 25 mph, top speed for many cars up to World War I, a windshield just got in the way, and side windows impaired one's hand-signals. Security? These rigs didn't even have keys, let alone locking mechanisms which would go off like Navy attack sirens when messed with.

When tops finally appeared in the 1900's, they weren't metal or wood, but canvas, burlap, bedsheet and airplane fabric—flimsy, drafty affairs as substantial as beach umbrellas and even more cantankerous to operate. Early cars had constant trouble in general, and the top, an experimental option, was no exception. But this fact was accepted as inherent to the car, the way the vote was inherently a male privilege; few people gave it a thought.

Before 1910, almost all cars were: 1) custom designed and 2) ragtops. The car was neither a necessity nor a commonplace, but an expression of worth and a projection of the individual personality of the owner. Mass-production was still a gleam in Ford's eye, and "automakers" were really just assemblers of parts collected from many scattered sources. In 1903, Neustadt-Perry advertised its Genevieve Runabout thusly: "You Can Build It Yourself." Or you could tell the assembler what you wanted and he would put it together for you. When Duryea promised "Automobile Vehicles of All Kinds," they meant *all*. Each car was unique—a roll-your-own automobile created like modern stereo systems, out of components and to specifications. Up to 1908, handwork was considered better than machinework, and the result was

BUBBLE
NUMBER

Life

PRICE **10** CENTS
VOL. LIX, NO. 1523.   JANUARY 4, 1912
COPYRIGHT, 1912, LIFE PUBLISHING COMPANY

THE LATEST MODEL

"THEY SHALL INHERIT THE EARTH"

a tide of display-cases on wheels.

It was the Age of the Roadster—gaudy concoctions, all brass and vigor, which combined the elegant enormity of the limousine with the handling and two-seat cockpit feeling of the sports car. They were manifestly status symbols, and anyone who could own one, did. The roadster was considered almost incapable of improvement, and therefore changes were minor: the cabriolet version replaced the basic roadster's fold-down windshield with a fixed one and the more primtive curtains with roll-up side windows; the Phaeton version was just a four-door, but basic roadie lines went unchanged.

Then came 1908, a year of ominous portent for the open car. General Motors was founded, and the Model T was born. Mass-production had arrived, and with it the death knell of the custom automobile. Cars would no longer be uniquely characteristic but as identical as possible. The T—the most successful car ever built in America and the harbinger of the auto industry as we know it—still had a cloth top. But precisely because the open car now flooded the roads, it became common. And so, when the 1908 Franklin brougham offered a permanent metal roof, the auto-

mobile family branched out for the first time.

Instead of "the car," there were now "the Roadster" and "the Sedan." The former had a lowerable cloth top and often side curtains instead of windows. The latter were enclosed by metal and glass. They were named to reflect a division in the way we drove: the roadster was for traveling down the open road; the sedan was for being carried through the city streets. A 1910 Olds Special ad illustration showing a capped-and-goggled driver racing alongside a train became the world's most famous auto picture; it was tacked on men's club walls everywhere. It was what the roadster was all about. By contrast, Buick was promoting the new, enclosed "Body by Fisher" as the perfect vehicle to carry the family to church. This was what the sedan was all about. Given this division, the car assumed new social significance. There were now Road People and Street People, and although these two types were hardly new, there was now a handy, portable way for both elements to advertise the distinction. The roadster symbolized youth, daring, flare. The sedan symbolized affluence, maturity, caution. The automotive caste system had begun. We will see more of it.

SILENCE · *Peerless* · COMFORT

ALL THAT THE NAME IMPLIES

"48-Six" Six-passenger Torpedo

Entrance to
Hotel St. Regis
New York

Of those material things having to do with the art of good living, there is rightly expected beauty, richness, and refinement. In a fine motor car, to produce pleasurable ease in riding, they must be combined with usefulness founded in a smooth-running mechanism.

The Peerless Motor Car Company
Cleveland, Ohio
Makers also of Peerless Commercial Cars

JIM: I think I will have to get a new car.
WILL: What's wrong with the one you have?
JIM: I can't pay for it.

GOODBYE GREAT OUTDOORS.]

THE VERY CONCEPT of the car had changed by the 1920's. Ford's success formula involved designing a car for the *mass market*; something durable, simple, and inexpensive. This formula, which would eventually doom such eccentricities as the ragtop, put over 15,000,000 Model T's on the highways. The car was no longer a luxury, but a family item. The difference was major.

Previously, cars had been jewels, even purchased as such. You sat down with an individual craftsman and translated your imagination into automotive design. Your tastes weren't randomly sampled, researched and averaged out into three or four basic models. Nobody else had the same car. Naturally you wanted it to be seen in. Now you might still call them jewels, but they no longer issued forth from some automotive Tiffany's—rather from the Woolworth's of the motorcar, the Ford Company. There were accessories to be chosen, but every basic unit was identical, and the effect was more charm bracelet than precious gem. What had been exciting, exclusive and romantic became mundane and proletarian. Almost

anybody could own a car with a cloth top; you could get a 1926 Model A for $290. Alas, a cheap car made you a cheap driver by association.

As long as hardtops weren't being cheaply mass-produced, the average man couldn't simply buy one off the rack, and the sedan's extra cost made it the preserve of affluence. But no sooner had metal tops achieved the grace of status than the 1922 Hudson offered a closed car for just $100 more than its open model. Steel-enclosed status, too, would soon be within the grasp of multitudes and would begin changing us from a nation of ragtoppers to one of hardtoppers.

Motoring had been in its adventuresome stage from 1905–1920. The sedan now tamed it. The cloth car was charming, true; but the metal car became the one to own. Of all the hardtop's real or imagined advantages, this would prove the most formidable: not just that it was quieter, less aromatic and immune to the elements—which it was—but that it was *respectable*. From this point on, the ragtop increasingly became a subsection of the auto industry.

Fine ladies had much leisure in the age of chivalry—their needlework was often a lasting artistic achievement

The Dietrich Convertible Sedan

CULTURED women instinctively recognize and appreciate fine work—whether it be the decorator's, the modiste's or the motor car designer's.

The preference such women have shown for Packard cars—not in a few large centers only but in every section of the Union—is a tribute to three particularly well recognized Packard qualities, beauty, prestige and long life.

For women wish the family car and particularly their own private cars to reflect good taste and discrimination inside and out, to possess a distinguished reputation and, withal, to be of good quality and lasting service.

Woman recognizes a Packard—either Six or Eight—to be something more than a mere utility. She sees it also as a work of art. Here is necessary transportation made luxurious—and clothed with beauty.

The very needlework, and there is much of it hidden in the soft upholstery of a Packard interior, reflects the pride which Packard women take in aiding to produce the best built car in the world.

PACKARD
ASK THE MAN WHO OWNS ONE

One Car for Riding and a Spare Car for Parking.

"Don't get excited, Martha. Our chauffeur used to be an aviator, he'll manage it all right."

At the end of World War I, less than ten per cent of all cars on the road had solid roofs, but mass-production and unitized-construction tooling quickly changed that. If nothing else, a piece of canvas thrown over a car had been inexpensive. Now, a steel shell up there cost little more. When this manufacturing capacity merged with economic imperatives and the public's growing fondness for comfort and privacy, the hardtop held an unbeatable hand.

The '20s introduced more changes. Emphasis on design and technology gave way to emphasis on promotion and economics, the classic shift from craftsmanship to industry. This trend was most notable in advertising. The auto race—the car's original form of promotion—had stressed the speed and flare of the product. Now, magazine ads took over. You couldn't show velocity on the printed page as graphically as you could portray luxury and comfort. Thus car ads began concentrating not on driving itself, but on the snug ways of doing so. Convenience started to compete with verve.

By the mid-'20s, the car was big business, concentrated in major industrial centers. This produced an urban bias toward practicality which would forever weigh against the open car. The non-cranked electric starter was introduced and created an entirely new market—the woman driver. Bad news for the clothtop: coiffures and other feminine trappings now had to be considered by auto designers. Ladies would soon be half of the car-buying public and did not cotton to rolling wind tunnels. Convenience and safety became the big selling points. The industry built and sold accordingly.

Overnight, the name of the game was comfort. Smoother interstate highways, the balloon tire and roll-up windows all catered to this trend. The advent of the sedan also meant that scores of accessories became not only feasible, but desirable: radios, heaters, overhead lights, lush interiors; the business bloomed with *options*, high-markup items which allowed auto dealers to afford silk ties and large homes. Each option was sold separately, with its own extra profit-margin, and most were more practical and protected in a hardtop. Not surprisingly, the closed car was hyped, extolled and marketed with religious vim by the entire auto industry, whose powers of persuasion are second only to gunpoint. At this point, when the *economic* leverage had shifted to metaltops, the open car's days were numbered.

Life

Automobile Number

January 14 1928   Price 15 cents

Driver's License

N

FATIGUED FREDDIE: Dusty, I guess ye're right. A closed car is de t'ing nowadays.

The times also produced a disastrous social phenomenon: the car was found to play a vital function in facilitating the act of fornication, and in the '20s it became a portable hotel room without the vexations of registration, cost or exposure. This was something adolescents had been waiting for since Queen Victoria. It struck a greater blow for sexual freedom, or at least the brief expression thereof, than anything short of the Pill. The back seat was far preferable to the front porch, and suddenly the car wasn't just your mode of transportation, but your destination as well.

If there is any stronger motivation in America than the force of sex, industry in general and advertising in particular would like to hear about it. Society has yet to create an institution which can stand against the momentum of the loins, and the ragtop was no exception. An enclosed car was a private car, which is to say a mobile bedchamber. As such, the enclosed car was suddenly illicit, and thus *sexy*. It was also a comfortable car, a major factor in light of the effects of winter night air on exposed anatomical delicacies. Thus, the hardtop became the strategic hamlet of the cheap thrill—which is the most saleable kind—and if there was any more important element working against the open car, it doesn't spring to mind.

But the soft top survived. In the '20s the car was still more of a social necessity than an economic one and America's major source of relaxation and recrea-

tion, and the ragtop was saved by prosperity and an era of high-living. The roadster became the theme car of the Roaring Twenties. At that time, the touring concept still dominated motoring, and this was the car for it. Everybody had the price of one, at least on paper, and it was the perfect insignia for a decade of indulgence. If the sedan was *sensible*, the ragtop was *popular*. Its advertising image involved lovely girls and dashing lads, not businessmen. It was the car we liked, in contrast to the one we needed. It drew attention and turned heads. Almost everyone admired it; hence flocks of people eagerly bought roadsters to be seen in.

The Stutz Bearcat was the ultimate expression of the Jazz Age, but the '20s waned with more varieties of clothtop than patent medicines—from $550 Model A's to $1795 Eclair Landaus to $13,500 J Duesenbergs. More like speedy, low-slung gypsy wagons than transportation, many were straight out of Jules Verne. There were no awkward limits to one's decorative imagination such as the graduated income tax, and words like "environment," "consumer," and "conservation" were found only in the dictionary; "ecology" and "conspicuous consumption" weren't even found *there*.

The road teemed with topless automotive dinosaurs crafted out of wood, steel, aluminum, you name it. Duesenbergs, Packards and Auburns dripped with

The New OAKLAND EIGHT

PRODUCT OF GENERAL MOTORS

For positive proof of its Superior Performance drive this car yourself

$1025 AND UP

Available in seven body types. Closed bodies by Fisher. Prices f. o. b. Pontiac, Mich., plus delivery charges

In your own community there are Oakland Eight owners who can tell you that Oakland is truly a car with Superior Performance. Yet no matter how convincing their statements, it is only by driving the car yourself that you can learn how exceptional Oakland's performance actually is. Take an Oakland Eight out on the highway and *prove to yourself* that few cars can equal its speed. *Prove to yourself* that scarcely a car you meet can match its remarkable power on the steepest hills. *Prove to yourself* that few cars, if any, are capable of the lightning acceleration which sends

Oakland ahead like a flash. *Prove to yourself* that Oakland's 85-horsepower V-type engine, developing one horsepower to 37 pounds of car weight, has raised eight-cylinder performance to an entirely new level among cars selling around $1000. . . . *Get positive proof* that General Motors' lowest-priced eight is a car with Superior Performance, by driving an Oakland Eight yourself. Your local Oakland-Pontiac dealer will gladly place a car at your disposal, without obligating you in any way. . . . Oakland Motor Car Company, Pontiac, Michigan.

superior performance

Write for interesting booklet which illustrates and describes the design of the New Oakland Eight

"There's something wrong. This gear-shift doesn't work."
"That isn't the gear-shift, Jack. It's—er—it's my knee."

every imaginable feature, from rear-seat windshields to hand-cranked retractable headlights. These colossal projectiles—half car, half calliope—were up to 20 feet long, had engines as big as coffins with the cumulative power of up to 800 horses, and could hurl themselves around at 140 mph. Indeed, they were as close as you could get to flying a plane without actually leaving the ground. The limousine was pompous, the sedan drab, the sports car a dangerous extravagance. But the roadster was a class act, with the best features of all.

And for those who could afford one and who looked even halfway human, there had never been a tool of seduction like the roadster. Anybody who didn't look sexy in an Auburn Boattail Speedster belonged in a sideshow. The roadie was expensive, exciting, exotic, extroverted, *fun*. Women looked at it and something magical and Pavlovian happened.

Nevertheless, whereas there had been nine open cars sold for every closed one in 1919, in 1929 the figures were exactly the reverse. The '20s would be the ragtop's last real hurrah. By 1927, its very lines were being rounded and patterned after hardtop styling, until they were no longer open-road cars, but mere sedans with lowerable tops—"convertible sedans," to be exact. The introduction of this designation completed the transition from the distinct roadster *line* to the new convertible sedan *option*. The ragtop as such had been sent to the minors.

Gradually, the unequivocal roadster concept was displaced by this bet-hedging half-breed. The new convertible was a minor sales smash, in fact, and established itself with two specific buying markets which would continue to sustain it from then on—the young, or those who wished to appear so; and closet joyriders from the upper brackets. When the roadster died out in 1929, the convertible had terminated the open car as a breed of its own. Within four years sedan lines had blown the roadster lines off the showroom floors.

The convertible then inherited the symbolism of the speed, dash and whoopie of ragtime motoring, the car's highest form of jubilation and dazzle. The convert became the top of the carmaker's line—speedsters and cabriolets with 130-inch wheelbases and net weights of two tons were the glaze on the upper crust. They signified not just status but *élan*, rather like some combination of the Porsche Targa and Continental Mark V might have today, if such a crossbreed were possible. The convertible was the state-of-the-art of automotive elitism; the working definition of class and distinction; the premiere achievement of design, quality and craftsmanship; and it carried a price tag that would stop your heart.

The Bugatti Royale 41 was as big as a PT boat—the hood alone wasn't much smaller than a Vega—and cost 30 grand before you even got past the chassis to the customized body. The 1930 Packard convert could be had from the factory for $5200; a heady sum even today, it was enough to make a car buyer see spots at the time, and such items were only family cars if the family's name was DuPont. But then came the Crash and people on ledges, and everything went into the sink, including the auto industry, which got clobbered. Hardest hit were the grandiose open-car toys of the aristocracy. Insofar as sudden paper wealth went the way of the whooping crane, so by and large did they.

HARD CHOICES, HARD TOPS.⟧

THE CONVERTIBLE WAS the first compromise between hardtop logic and clothtop emotion. Being an option, the open car was now a choice, and thus a designation. Its diminishing numbers made it special: a thing of glamor, rakishness, *savoir faire*. Whoever desired those qualities—and they ranged from Mafiosi to Nobel laureates to FDR —rode in a car with the top down.

The connie was most popularized by that dynamo of romanticism, the motion picture. Hollywood absolutely loved the idea of a car whose top could be lowered, and not simply because ragtop ownership was so completely *de rigueur* among the top stars of the '30s. Hollywood took to the rag like a duck to another duck because it was visual, dashing and glamorous, and because no other vehicle, given a simple

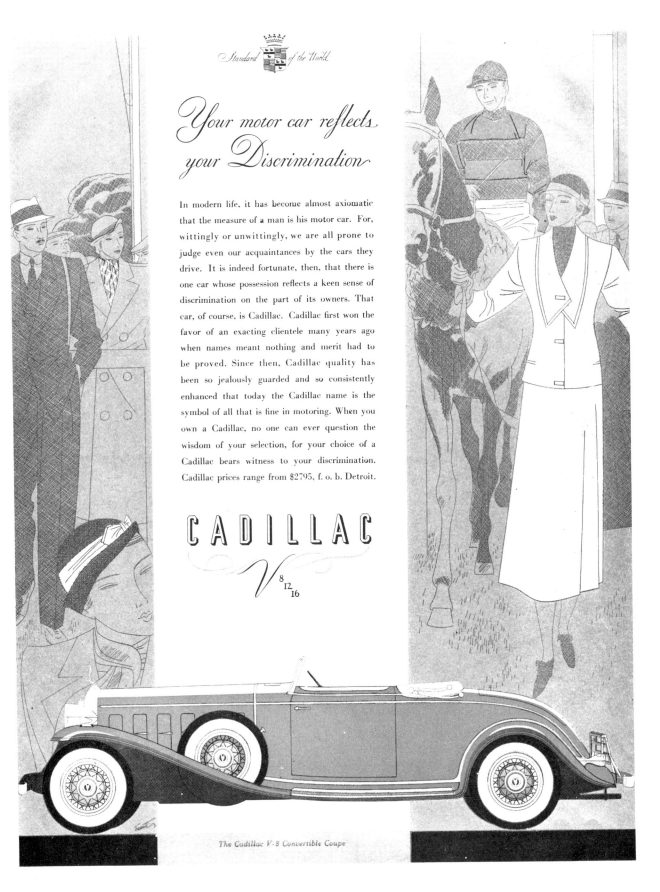

soundstage and a wind machine, could so immediately convey the idea of speed, danger and vicarious excitement. It was matchlessly photogenic and made lighting a snap. Nothing had been so difficult to illuminate properly for the cameras as a car interior. Cramped, dark and concealing, the closed auto literally had to be sawed in half to be filmable. Not so the convert. Interior, head-on and overhead shots were a cinch with no metal roofs and side panels to contend with. You could see the actors clearly and effortlessly. You could run the wind through their hair, have them laughing and yelling in the breeze, and doing interesting things like standing up, or jumping out, or dropping into the car from above, or leaping aboard when it was already moving. To a director, the convert was a *carte blanche* on wheels. To a performer, it became a virtual necessity.

In hardtops you saw grocers, families, deacons, salesmen and plumbers. In convertibles you saw every icon of glamor in America—Cary Grant, Kate Hepburn, Mary Pickford, John Barrymore, Carole Lombard, Clark Gable, Jean Arthur, Gary Cooper, Myrna Loy, Spencer Tracy, Ginger Rogers, Humphrey Bogart, *ad celebritum*. Today, if you want to identify with a Redford, Dunaway, Nicholson or Streisand, you'd better have the price of a Mercedes just to start with. In the 1930's you could approximate the style in which our self-projected idols roamed around for a few grand. A ton of fantasies were staged in the topless auto, and a ton of same were indulged by anyone who could afford one, and by many who could not. Instant make-believe.

The vinyl boot behind the rear seat was more than a handy place to store the top. It was also another row of seats for those who threw caution and cosmetics to the winds. The passing world became a kind of wide-

HEADSTART TO HAPPINESS!

Now's the time and here's the car to make your dreams come true . . . The Buick CENTURY Series 60 Convertible Coupe, $1135 list at Flint, Mich.

YOU know a straight white road where the new leaves wait to whisper in the breeze of your passing.

You know a pretty girl with laughter-ready lips, and an eagerness to taste the fresh caress of a soft spring night upon her cheek.

Take your pretty girl, and on that moon-splashed road let the Century tell its own quiet-voiced story of power and steadiness and even-keeled comfort.

Feel the surge of its take-off, the smoothness of its swing into speed. Sample the swerveless firmness of its tiptoe hydrau-

lics, its instant responsiveness to your hands on the wheel. Test the perfect balance of it, unspoiled by jerk, shiver, strain or rubbery jumpiness—and find a motoring thrill that needs no touch of hazard to give it spice.

Not long since the winds were howling and the roads were glazed with ice. Now you have spring nights, clear roads, a headstart to the happiness that should be yours this summer in a Buick Century.

Isn't this the time to see this brilliant new Buick—and drive it—and decide to have one for your own?

NO OTHER CAR IN THE WORLD HAS ALL THESE FEATURES

Valve-in-Head Straight-Eight Engine . . . Anolite Pistons . . . Sealed Chassis . . . Luxurious "Turret Top" Body by Fisher with Fisher No Draft Ventilation . . . Tiptoe Hydraulic Brakes . . . Knee-Action Comfort and Safety . . . Torque-Tube Drive . . . Automatic Starting, Spark and Heat Control . . . Built-in Luggage Compartments . . . Front-End Ride Stabilizer

★ ★ ★ ★

$765 to $1945 are list prices of the new Buicks at Flint, Mich. Standard and special accessories groups at extra cost

Buick 8
A GENERAL MOTORS PRODUCT

★ ★ ★ ★ WHEN BETTER AUTOMOBILES ARE BUILT, BUICK WILL BUILD THEM ★ ★ ★ ★

screen movie, and if the ragtop was the theater of the road, its boot was the balcony. It was the traditional seat of honor at every self-respecting parade, from Tournament of Roses to ticker-tape, and above all it made the connie more a *ride* than a mere conveyance. The appropriate descriptive phrase, in fact, was "joyriding"—seldom heard any more, partly because riding is no longer a joy, and partly because the vehicle it was coined for is no longer made.

The Depression might have scuttled the convert altogether, but for two vital groups. The first was the poor, of whom there was no apparent end, and for whom the mass-produced ragtop, cheaper than the sedan model, was the only possibility. The second was the remaining rich, for whom, as a flamboyantly conspicuous extravagance, it was the display car. If you still had it, there was no better way to flaunt it than in a Cord, Duesenberg, or Cadillac Phaeton. If you didn't have it, at least the $430 Model A and $650 Chevy Independence converts took less of it than hardtops. Items like the $795 Pontiac connie coupe even managed to wring a profit from the ravaged middle class. The ragtop hung in there.

Nothing produces pragmatism like hard times, however, and this accelerated the shift in priorities and consciousness from flare and styling toward engineering economy and efficiency. Horsepower ratings rose, as did auto speeds, while appearance was relatively ignored. Durability became a watchword; frills were dispensed with. Turnpikes flourished, and though they were "open roads," they carried drivers through changing climates, well into the night, and at hurricane speeds. You now flowed alongside three other lanes of cars. You didn't flash through the surroundings; you *were* the surroundings.

The car was no longer a plaything, but a practicality. The 1934 Ford was typical—enclosed, with smooth corners and tiny windows—designed not for touring, but stop-and-go driving and foul weather. The themes of streamlining and maximum enclosure would predominate through the early post-war models of 1949, and the sun would not be rediscovered until the '50s.

New features such as the automatic transmission and air conditioning (1938) illustrated the trend toward convenience, a characteristic the ragtop wasn't known for. It was chilly, loud, did little to exclude the noxious hydrocarbons poured out by early exhaust systems, and was definitely not all-weather. The "one-man" top was a common phrase in auto adver-

The 1936 Packard 12 Convertible Victoria pictured before the Sleepy Hollow Country Club

New York's Westchester prefers Packards

A SURVEY of fine car registrations in New York's smart suburban area of Westchester reveals Packard as predominant. Nearly 50 per cent of the fine cars owned in Westchester today are Packards—a significant tribute to the distinguished and distinctive Packard lines.

And this is simply a reflection of the nationwide trend. During the past twelve months, nearly half of all the fine cars purchased in America have been Packards.

Many of the purchasers are among the more than a thousand distinguished American families who have driven Packards continuously for twenty-one years or more.

For twenty years Mrs. R. Clifford Black, the owner of this magnificent home on the Boston Post Road, Pelham Manor, has also owned Packards. Socially prominent, she today enjoys the services of two Packard Twelves and two Packard Eights.

Above is the charming Colonial home of Norman Rockwell, on Lord Kitchener Road, New Rochelle. He is, of course, the nationally known artist and a Packard owner for many years.

The home of John Motley Morehead, former U. S. Minister to Sweden, on Forest Avenue, Rye. Mr. Morehead now has three Packard Super Eights —has been a Packard owner for thirty-one years.

PACKARD

EIGHT
SUPER-EIGHT
TWELVE

Ask the man who owns one

KEITH KIMBALL
AND HIS
"HAWAIIAN GOOKS"

1935

tising, but more ballyhooed than actually seen. Supposedly, it could be raised and lowered without aid, but great was the frustration generated in anyone taking this claim seriously. Most one-man tops were raised and lowered without annoyance only by two civil engineers on laudanum. The convertible became viewed as cumbersome and inconvenient.

The 1930's also saw the rise of a dimension which would eventually dominate, define and determine future automotive development: the car was simultaneously creating and becoming the vehicular mainstay of the *commuter*. For openers, this routinized driving. Celebration—the spirit of holiday and boundlessness—doesn't come easy from something you spend two hours a day in, five days a week, almost none of which is inspiring. The car grew mundane, a symbol of boring necessity, and those looking for the zing and blam of life went elsewhere. Further,

the commute car was now beginning to run *us*. It had to be serviceable and comfortable year-round, regardless of climate or hour. The choice was between enclosure on a nice spring Sunday in a hardtop, or 40-minute crawls through driving rain or snow a dozen times a winter in a clothtop. Hardly a contest.

In freezing traffic jams, there was nothing like the hermetic environment of steel while others around you shivered in their wheeled tents to convey a sense of superiority. In the world of the commuter, the hardtop consolidated its image of affluence. A cloth top was now something we *had* to put up or take down. A joy had become a chore. From this point on, the original classic motor car—the clothtop—would go into a sales and production decline which would be almost a straight line from pre-eminence to oblivion. It wouldn't give up—or be given up—easily, though, and would cling to life for 45 years.

"Gee, Bill, that eight's the smoothest thing I ever saw!"
"Which eight?"

Eight cylinders for smoothness . . . and ECONOMY

Most people know that eight cylinders make a smoother, quieter, sweeter running engine than any lesser number of cylinders.

But not every one realizes that good design may also make eight cylinders more economical. Ford has proved the fact twice in 1937.

The 85-horsepower Ford V-8 engine—long famous for its flashing performance—now gives greater gasoline economy than ever. Owners report averages of 17-21 miles per gallon.

The 60-horsepower Ford V-8 engine—tested for two years in England and France before its American introduction—has established itself as the most economical Ford engine ever built! Careful cost records from owners show averages of 22-27 miles per gallon.

Choose between these modern engines by their power and your purse. Both are built into the same handsome, husky, comfortable car. Both, because of their compact V-type construction, provide extra

room for you and your luggage. Both are low priced. In fact, the "60" is available in five standard body types at the lowest Ford price in years!

Ford V·8

AS LONG AS IT'S OLIVE-DRAB.⟧

B Y THE END of the '30s, America's pre-war industrial gearing-up had created jobs, a revived new-car market and a new and different look in automotive styling. In 1940 we were buying great massive metal shells, better suited for battering down walls than getting a tan. Some of the cars were little more than rolling bunkers with a window here and there, reflecting both a changing social attitude and a corporate re-tooling which reeked of war-cloud psychology. We were getting ready to build tanks, and you could see the future in the ominous styling.

Every worthwhile American carmaker still offered at least one ragtop and often a stylistic and financial variety, from the huge Lincoln Zephyr Continental cabriolet at $2840 to the tiny American Bantam at $525. In 1941 you could drive off the showroom floor in a $299 cloth-top Crosley only slightly bigger than a weevil. Even in 1940 dollars, this was close to theft, and could have made some auto history, resurrecting the convert as the basic American post-Depression economy car. But a few months after the model was introduced, greater history was made at Pearl Har-

bor, and for the next five years the automobile was filed under "Jeep" and the In look was military green.

In terms of auto evolution, the 1940's were mostly a blank page; the few passenger cars produced changed little. The industry went into suspended animation from 1941–1947, since the war put auto companies in the truck, tank, and aircraft businesses primarily. The orders of the day, as far as cars were concerned, were structural protection, huge horsepowers, quick acceleration and aerodynamic styling. Thus when the smoke cleared, Detroit was set up to produce vehicles emphasizing enclosure, safety and concealment.

This kind of car had a social life of its own in postwar America, and its sales accelerated parallel to our general shift in sentiment toward an era of mutual distrust and belligerence. We now called ourselves the Arsenal of Democracy, and the car increasingly became a mini-arsenal—of privacy, seclusion and individual isolationism on a par with our national thinking—and a vehicular deterrent to the invasion by others as well. The door lock and metal roof were

"Ford's out Front," says the Wise Old Owl

(AN INTERVIEW)

"I DON'T give a hoot for gimcracks," the Owl said, blinking, "I'm a practical man, I am, and I want a car that I can depend on. Now you take the 1947 Ford line—there are cars that suit me perfect and I'll tell you why.

"First, you get your choice of engines," and here he raised his eyebrows, "no other car in Ford's class lets you take your choice of either a V-8 or a Six.

"Then there's the matter of brakes," he went on. "They call 'em 'King-size' and that's what they be—with more braking area than any other car in Ford's class. The hydraulic feature makes 'em easy to apply, too!

"And, as to economy—well, I have a Scotch Grouse friend who tells me it's Ford's 4-ring aluminum pistons and balanced carburetion

"I never saw a more beautiful instrument panel," said Mrs. Owl.

that save a pretty penny on both gas and oil."

"But what about Ford BEAUTY," we asked. "Don't you have an eye for BEAUTY or are you too practical for that?"

"That's the wife's department," he replied solemnly, "but I can tell you she keeps me up days raving about Ford's longer, lower look, about the glamorous interiors and such. It's enough to drive a practical man mad."

"What are your views on safety?" we asked.

"If you are referring to Ford's 'Lifeguard' body I can tell you it's sound—really sound. But that's what you'd expect from the Ford people —thoroughly practical people. That's why Ford's out Front—and if you'd ask me I'd say they're out Front to stay!"

And with that, the Wise Old Owl blinked wisely and flew away!

"For savin' gas and oil ye canna beat 4-ring aluminum pistons," said the Scotch Grouse!

FORD'S OUT FRONT

There's a *Ford* in your future

[33]

our first line of defense; massive retaliation meant our car's ability to give more damage than it got in a collision situation. Words like "power" and "strength" replaced "luxury" and "flair." We dug bomb shelters, pulled the blinds, joined nothing; and we bought tinted glass and unit-body construction. The car, ever the most representative manifestation of American psychology, told the story. We pulled our heads back into our shell. We clamored for a nuclear umbrella and roll-bars at the same time, and for the same fundamental reasons. We were no longer headstrong and rash. We were nervous, suspicious, even fearful.

All this would surely have slain the ragtop but for a powerful counter-current. Wartime gas rationing had all but eliminated pleasure driving, a national 35-mph speed limit had taken the kick from the road, and car pools had jammed us together. The result was a post-war backlash of pent-up joyriders who couldn't wait to get away from it all on the highway. Some had given up the open car habit forever, but others lunged back into it.

The convertible prospered because for several years everything that could be put on four wheels prospered. This wasn't a trend, but a gold rush. The driver had been a virtual vehicular celibate for five years, frustrated to insatiability. The *second* person most returning GIs saw was male: a car dealer. Driving would become the cheapest, most popular and most symbolic enjoyment of the fruits of victory. The connie made a comeback. The war's end and the whirlwind prosperity following it were intense causes for a nationwide attitude of celebration, a function for which the ragtop had always seemed designed. The sedan still dominated the roadways, but the open car exemplified more than ever the Good Life of affordable leisure. Which was what we were fighting all those incessant wars for, after all. Along with swimming pools and split-levels, the convertible was conspicuous evidence of success and managed to hold its own as a commercial life-form going into the 1950's.

1950 RAMBLER CONVERTIBLE

THE '50S CAR was a victor's car, befitting the world's mightiest and most prosperous nation; a thing of clout and comfort, power brakes and steering, chrome and accessories. Our new individuality demanded and got a choice of engines, body styles, paint jobs, trim and interiors. Money talked, and nobody walked. Even the low-price jobs had 300 horsepower, and all were longer, sleeker, lower. Air conditioning and automatic transmissions were big-volume. We wanted power, creature comforts, convenience—all the fruits.

We also wanted glitter and splash. Unfortunately, *elegance* became confused with *gaudiness*. Groping for quality, we wound up embracing excess. Our idea of humor was Milton Berle, and our idea of automotive distinction was tailfins as big as sails. Rolling side-shows with clashing two-tone paint jobs, jutting edges and lights wherever possible were contrived in the name of prestige, and you often didn't know whether to salute or laugh. This national emphasis on filigree, furnishings and the showpiece-car kept the ragtop in style. But at this point in history it wasn't even a segment of the auto market; it was a segment of the *specialty* auto market. Which included custom cars, muscle cars, woodies, hotrods and foreign cars—all of them attempts to establish individuality in driving without actually having to display the individual. Innovations approximating the open car's attractions without suffering its vulnerability and inconvenience

burgeoned. Pillarless hardtop rooflines were introduced to maximize visibility and daylight; contrast-painted roofs gave the cosmetic illusion of a ragtop—both were efforts to lend the zest of convert styling to steelroofs. The 1957 Ford Skyliner carried this effort to preposterous extremes with a great retractable steel top operated by a byzantine mechanical apparatus which raised or lowered it into a trunk big enough to play ping pong in. People in Hollywood filming comedies loved this car, as did a few carbuyers, but almost nobody took it seriously.

Following the upheavals of the '30s and '40s, not much else could happen to the convertible in the '50s, and not much did. After the post-war boom, it fell back upon its hard-core market: the wealthy, who could afford a car reserved purely for frivolous activity; and teenagers, the majority of whose waking time was reserved purely for such activity. The rag-top was inherently adolescent and brazen, and the adolescent and brazen loved it.

The convertible again became synonymous with celebrities, heiresses, playboys and socialites. It had never *stopped* being synonymous with youth, through every teenage culture-image from Andy Hardy to Archie to James Dean. The definitive vehicle of the young had no top—remember—and was called the "jalopy." Always more form than function, it was now purely a plaything, for those well-heeled or still young enough to play.

This is the Eldorado—a new adventure in automotive design and engineering—with brilliant and dramatic styling . . . hand-crafted, imported leather interiors . . . "disappearing" top . . . and a sensational 270-h.p. engine. In all that it is, and does, and represents . . . it is the finest fruit of Cadillac's never-ending crusade to build greater quality into the American motor car.

Now in limited production • Price on request

Eldorado

BY CADILLAC

CADILLAC MOTOR CAR DIVISION • GENERAL MOTORS CORPORATION

Ragtops were big rolling toys: those of the rich came from Cadillac and Lincoln factories, reeked of leather and power options and were carefully priced to distinguish their owners from the *hoi polloi*; those of the young included the power of whole horse herds, were marvelously phallic and distinguished their owners from civilized man. Many of the former never even lowered the top—its presence was sufficient statement of earnings. Most of the latter never raised it—theirs were the very pace-cars of cruising, which demanded maximum exposure and a nine-passenger capacity (three on the rear window well).

For awhile, the suburbs teemed with connies—T-Birds and GTOs and Bel Airs. The car radio was a mobile rock-and-roll PA system, vital for Saturday night trolling. Drive-in everythings mushroomed. In this context, the convert was *hip*. Air conditioning was still a costly bauble, and when summer brought down broad stifling quilts of moist motionless air, the ragtop made more sense than Salk Vaccine. It was rakish without being punk. The hard-core low-rider element would have eliminated car windows altogether and welded the roof directly onto the doorframes if possible, but the open car, as associated with youth, was an impetuous but harmless phase. It was clean.

The convertible also established a sense of power and liberation very dear to suburb-trapped 1950's teenagers. Its ownership was usually the realization of a long-held desire; if your first car wasn't a convert, it was probably a disappointment. The top stayed down as long as there was anything even resembling sun in the sky. One imagined oneself the object of much envy by others, and one wasn't far off. One expected that young women of stimulating appearance would flock around, or at least show up in greater numbers than before, and one was usually right.

Then, after a seven-year splurge which saw prices go utterly amok, the auto boom crested at 8,000,000 new cars in 1955, so seriously flooding the market that demand dropped by 25 per cent in 1956, and a recession descended in 1957. Low-volume cars were the first to be cut back, and we emerged from this travail wanting less ornate bulk and more economy. Pragmatism geared up all over again and spat forth great torrents of that artless utility, the station wagon. Overnight, this dour antithesis to the ragtop was everywhere. Then came VW's immortal pregnant rollerskate and its call for America to "Think Small." Ultimately, a swarm of pocketbook-priced foreign cars blew away the last economic advantage of the convertible.

The VW was neither stylish, sporty, nor sexy. But it *worked*—suddenly, this fact was a big deal in light of accessory-groaning American mid-sizes, which also groaned with potential repair bills. Foreign car

1. The magic begins when you touch the button marked "Top". . .

2. Smoothly, electric motors lift the rear deck lid . . .

3. And then the top separates from the body . . .

4. Up and back goes the top. Front piece folds down . . .

5. Lower and lower sinks the top. Front piece tucks under . . .

6. Now the rear deck lid starts to lower itself . . .

7. Down . . . down . . . goes the deck lid . . .

8. And there you are . . . in the smoothest convertible ever!

Ford's introduction of the Skyliner, world's only all-steel hide-away hardtop, represents the beginning of a new era in automotive design. This *newest* new kind of Ford brings the motoring public the most exciting idea in automobile design since Ford presented the first two-door sedan in 1915.

If you are planning to buy *any* new car—no matter what kind—the fact that Ford created this car is important to you. For all the exhaustive research, planning and testing that went into the Skyliner is dramatic proof of the engineering skill you get in *every* Ford model.

So plan to see this history-making car, this prototype of a whole future generation of cars. It's ready for your own personal inspection now in the showrooms of many Ford Dealers. And ask your Dealer to show you the exciting advances in *all* models of the new Ford line for '57. For all the Skyliner's fabulous engineering is based on the very same "Inner Ford" that has proved the sensation of the industry in all 21 Ford models. These cars surround the rugged "Inner Ford" with the year's most successful styling—neither freakishly radical nor staidly conservative. And the heart of the "Inner Ford,"

of course, is its V-8 engine, made by the makers of 23,000,000 V-8's—more than all other car manufacturers *combined*.

Perhaps the most surprising news of all about this Ford Skyliner is its low price. A comparison of manufacturers' suggested retail prices shows only four "soft top" convertibles (including a Ford) are priced less than the Skyliner!

So plan to stop in soon and see your Ford Dealer. After you've watched this mechanical phenomenon go through its quick-change routine a few times, we believe you'll agree that a whole new age of automobiles begins with this car.

Seventh heaven on wheels—

imports went from 60,000 in 1955 to 700,000 in 1959, and collared ten per cent of the new-car market. To its credit, though, the Beetle clothtop kept the breed abundant beyond the abilities of American auto-makers for years.

Production of the connie was further stricken at this point by the *used car*, which became big business as those feeling the squeeze downshifted from the cheap new convertible to the cheaper used sedan or, even thriftier, the used ragtop. This last possibility particularly attracted the affection and limited funds of youth, whose high school/college environment demanded its flashy libertine presence. And the more used the car, the better. In contrast to the 1920's, when it was the staff-car of flaming youth, in the late '50s the ragtop was the angry young vehicle, the revel without a cause, a symbol of the rootlessness, alien-ation and unorthodoxy teenagers coveted. Old con-verts made noise, stank with fumes, limited vision with the top up and blew careful grooming all to hell with it down. The rear windows darkened and cracked, the tops disintegrated; but precisely because of all that, converts were the last pure automotive statement of cheek, brass and indifference and were *cool* beyond words.

Having lost the young and the poor, new-rag

makers concentrated on the rich, never a stupid de-cision. New-model converts became the flagships of many lines in the '50s, identified in the media with the elite. Their pricetags could break you faster than di-vorce; few sedans cost more. As it was the technique of advertising to glamorize car-ownership relent-lessly, convertibles became the customary model-draped centerpiece in magazines and on TV. When it came to buying, the sedan still swept the field, but the lascivious clothtop was a superb shill for drawing buyers into the showroom.

Two quintessential convertibles were introduced as attempts to lure the sports car crowd—the Cor-vette and Thunderbird—but they attracted as many clothtoppers to the sports car as the reverse, and countless faces previously windblown now turned Europeward for their kicks, to a toy whose cost ap-pealed to the rich and whose sexiness to the young and hormonal. It virtually replaced the rag at the college level, and young lawyers who formerly took Sunliners to the beach now drove there in MGs. As the '50s ended, the connie was fighting a holding ac-tion. There would be isolated periods of vigor, but the patient was a hopeless case. It was just a matter of when to pull the economic plug.

The new kind of Ford for '57 brings yonder up close!

LONG, LEAN AND PACKED WITH PUNCH

Ford goes big...Ford goes low...Ford goes lively... in 2 big new sizes, each with the touch of tomorrow.

Here is the longest, lowest, heaviest, biggest low-priced car *ever*. You'll feel like a millionaire just having it parked out front. It's designed so grandma can get in and out easy as pie—so a lanky Texan has leg and head room to spare.

But, even more important, here's a car that's built to stay *built*, no matter what the years and the miles dish out. For the completely new Inner Ford has built-in extra quality to *keep* that wonderful new-car feel.

What's more, you get up to 245 hp in the new Silver Anniversary V-8's. It's mightier power that has been trained to live on a leaner-than-ever gas diet. And if you want *real* thrift, try Ford's new Mileage Maker Six, America's most modern "Six." *Six or V-8, the going is great.*

And you'll find just the Ford for you among the over-16-foot Custom and Custom 300 models, the over-17-foot Fairlane and Fairlane 500 models, or the Station Wagon Series with its five new glamour cruisers.

Best of all, all Fords are priced with the lowest! Come in today—meet the car that makes luxury a low-priced word.

It's fun to go first with **Ford**

NEW SUN AND FUN CAR!!! CORVAIR MONZA CONVERTIBLE

ROLLING OR OTHERWISE.⟧

THIS WOULD BE the last full decade of life for the convertible. Our driving environment would change drastically, and natural selection would not favor the open car. Pollution—already a major concern—would do as much to kill it off as anything. One no longer enjoyed the smell or consistency of the air that blew in one's face, and sales of cars with air conditioning lept from 11 per cent of the market in 1962 to 55 per cent in 1969.

Curving roads and lush scenery were no longer why we drove and were increasingly unavailable anyway. Whereas small-town tedium had been fled in gregarious mobility, urban congestion was fled in hasty solitude, preferably of the airtight pleasure-chamber variety. Rush-hour traffic did anything but rush and became so grim, rank and frustrating that the more you could blot it out, the better. The highways were scant improvement. If we couldn't wait to get into our cars, we also couldn't wait to get out of them. Motorists were now invariably *going* somewhere, not just killing time. The drive was not an end, merely a troublesome means to real escape—parks, campgrounds, lakes, mountains. The open car had been an interface with our surroundings, but now the goal was to insulate us from them, specifically from the eight-lane dreariness of freeways. An entire subtechnology was fired up to salvage this dead time,

or at least pass it as quickly and obliviously as possible. Tape decks and AM-FM radios sold like crazy.

Ironically, a sharp blow to the ragtop in the latter '60s was dealt by a spiritual compatriot—rock and roll. For the first time, the *fidelity* of a car radio became a matter of serious concern. You got hooked on the stone resonance of stereo at home and were suddenly bereaved by its absence on the road. 1950's rock could be listened to in a laundromat, but Beatles-era sound required clear reproduction, huge volume and at least two speakers. But nothing was so pointless and unsatisfying as $500 worth of sound evaporating tinnily away into air moving 65 mph—the speed limit back then, and a velocity particularly suited to the rhythms of jackhammer rock. Furthermore, in city traffic the soft top was porous to every available dissonant noise. Even parked in the garage, a convertible couldn't offer acoustics which matched those provided by the seal of steel and insulation.

Additionally, the rise of auto sound systems made sidewalk thieves everywhere lick their lips. Why strip the engine when the Blaupunkt gear was worth more and easier to get at? Solid-state treasure, protected by no more than a piece of fabric, was just a switchblade away. For more than a few people, the choice between rag and rock wasn't difficult. The highspeed blast and sweeping rush once provided by

Chevelle Malibu Super Sport Convertible in Goldwood Yellow.

STYLING THAT MOVES YOU EVEN WHEN IT'S STANDING STILL

If you ever can catch a Chevelle that's not on the go, look over its bold, exciting lines and sumptuous interior. It's The Chevelle Look—all new, already classic!

Note, for example, the graceful fender sweep, front to rear. Lamps blending gently into an unbroken total design above the massive rear wraparound bumper. The tastefully restrained use of trim, front, side and rear.

See how functional each crisp detail can be, too! Curved side glass is stylish, yet adds to the generous interior room. 115-inch wheelbase is jaunty, also makes handling and parking virtually effortless. Rich fabrics and handsome vinyls add interior beauty—and comfort. In

coupes and sedans, the squared-off rear window is extremely smart and allows maximum vision.

Eleven beautiful Chevelles, including convertibles, sport coupes, sedans and wagons, offer true Chevrolet value at moderate cost. See them at your Chevrolet dealer's. Test-drive one or two of them while you're there, too.

They'll move you with their styling—and with just about any measure of six or V8 power you like. . . . Chevrolet Division of General Motors, Detroit, Michigan.

Chevrolet • Chevelle • Chevy II • Corvair • Corvette

THE GREAT HIGHWAY PERFORMERS

CHEVELLE! BY CHEVROLET

[[43]]

wind in our faces now came instead in a wall of sound. And it didn't stop whenever the car did.

By the mid-'60s, the luxury-convertible market had diminished so dramatically that clothtops were only offered by topline models, whose reputation required that they provide any option their clientele could pay for. As for the youth market, it had simply fallen apart. The ragtop's hedonism and frivolity were incompatible with a period of *jungepolitik* which took itself extremely seriously. The convertible was a trinket of wealthy extravagance. It was wasteful and unecological. The van was more bohemian, the compact car more practical, the motorcycle more adventurous, the truck earthier, the VW more proletarian. The prevailing image of the clothtop was macho beefcake cars, high-performance Firebirds and Malibus. Long hair and 60 mph windspeeds got along poorly.

Indeed, the last healthy breath for the open car was the mid-range, heavy-firepower unit with four-on-the-floor and mag rims. The ragtop was still America's cruisemobile, but more and more persons under 25 were doing their cruising pharmaceutically or on

the stump for McCarthy. The clothtop's last stand turned out to be as the display car of the young working unmarried moderate American—the Singles Car. This wasn't ignominious, but logical. Insulation and airtight interiors had eliminated all semblance of motion but the visual, which was little more than evidence, let alone the feeling, of speed. What good were those 348 horses in that mill if you couldn't hear or feel or even smell them, if you couldn't get all that sensory input a Plymouth Sport Fury could generate blown into your face at 96 feet per second?

Reprieved by the singles power-car market, the connie's last good year was 1965, with 510,000 sales. In many ways, it was the *country's* last good year, followed by riots, the war, protest, dope, Watergate, oil hikes, slumps and shortages. Hereafter, the grandiose techno-flash of the 1960's became excess baggage. Screw prestige; we wanted *value*. Costs of upkeep and insurance became sobering issues, and compacts and subcompacts arrived in blizzards from Detroit and abroad. Belts were tightened in earnest, and the ragtop was an early notch. This was no time for frills.

BUT IT ONLY LASTED WHILE IT WAS FUN.⟧

WITH THE 1970's, we entered into the post-affluent age, meaning everyone had rather less money than he expected and far less than he wanted. When austerity hit the white-collar singles, that was it. Screaming inflation and fuel crises made the rag's showy capriciousness somehow crass, a statement of selfish indifference. It wasn't particularly wasteful or unecological, but the self-indulgent spirit it represented was growing *unfashionable*, and nothing will kill a display-mechanism quicker.

The '70s also began amid rampant consumerism and an almost neurotic safety-consciousness which tended to view *conceivable* threats to life and limb as *imminent* ones. The rag is no hermetic chamber or armored car. It is vulnerable. In an era when it was widely suggested that Detroit had more ways to kill us than Russia, the idea of playing into their hands via some topless deathtrap became folly. There's a big difference between the idea that a sane man shouldn't drive a ragtop and the idea that nobody should; but the latter notion was in vogue, and the movement to protect us from ourselves strove mightily for seatbelts, airbags, and an end to such suicidal heresies as cars uncovered with metal.

Finally, there was crime—a bumper crop, it seemed. Especially where clothtopped cars were concerned. Street burglary and sheer vandalism were veritable cottage industries in the cities, as random pointless destruction became a growing side-effect of life everywhere; and the connie's fragility and rarity became too much for any self-respecting destructo-looter to resist.

In 1970, open car sales were at 92,000 and dropping like stone. It had gone the way of James Bond extravagance, cheap gas, safe streets and short hair. The new asceticism had arrived. Inundated by govern-

Determination has its rewards.

A tradition of building great cars like the 1933 Cadillac 355 Phaeton has its advantages—and rewards—for today's luxury car buyer. First, we stubbornly maintain that a luxury car should be a thing of beauty. This is reflected in all nine Cadillacs—including Eldorado, the only American-built luxury convertible. Then, there's Total Cadillac Value. Because of it, Cadillac resale is traditionally the highest of any U.S. luxury car make...and its repeat ownership the greatest of any U.S. car make. Cadillac. **Then and Now...an American Standard for the World.**

Cadillac '75

ment safety and economy regulations, the auto industry saw handwriting on every wall in its house. The rag was still legal but increasingly difficult to market against a social tide, and Detroit's policy became "live-and-let-die." In 1965, one new car in 18 had been open; by 1972 it was less than one in 100. Convertibles weren't even shown in some catalogs, let alone in the ads.

Low sales phased the connie out of line after line. Nova, Falcon and Valiant converts had already disappeared when American Motors called it a day in 1968. Chrysler threw in the towel in 1971; Ford followed in 1973. In 1974 GM offered a half-dozen connies as options on their topline luxury models, but they actually sold fewer than 28,000 of them—less than one per cent of total auto sales, a figure automakers round off to *none*. At this level you're talking either novelties or loss-leaders, and Detroit had time for neither.

1976. America celebrated its 200th year of independence more dependent than ever on such acquired needs as peace and quiet, comfort, convenience, safety, luxury and personal space. Excitement, daring, display and status could easily be bought else-

where, or vicariously, or ignored altogether. Caddy bought up the last collapsing mechanisms on the market, and their 14,000th unit, the last American ragtop, drove off the line in April. So much for that.

In the case of the convertible there was no single smoking gun; no handy villain such as cheerless Detroit designers, environmental overkill, social paranoia or winter in Buffalo. Its demise was both simple and complex. It's gone because there wasn't sufficient desire for it to justify the expense of making it, but this breaks down to countless tiny changes in day-to-day reality which nicked away at the open car the way the press nicked away at Nixon. One day its support was gone; the next day so was it.

But let us not indulge that heroin of the emotions, nostalgia. The convertible raced and sang; it also clattered and stank. It was full of life; it could also kill you. If the car with the cloth roof is to be mourned, at least mourn it with dignity, as you would a loved one. Be glad that we had it at all, not to mention over 76 years, and that it gave us so much pleasure that we regret its loss.

Every car should do so much.

THIS WAS THE MUSTANG'S first model year and also the hottest collector's car in the series. Those built after 1971 featured a lower, fatter body style not considered "classic," but probably better in terms of power and comfort. It's one of the few really "bulletproof" cars; meaning almost nothing bad can be said of one (although you could fishtail one on your own spit). Basically in spirit and styling the early Mustangs were convertibles which also came in a sedan model. The last cloth Mustang in 1973 *was* the basic model, and the sedan just an optional version called the Grande. Gail Roulund of Oakland got this one virtually new, a six-month-old repossession. It's had a ring job and a new muffler, and now runs "gorgeously," with 122,000 miles. She's a non-collector; in fact, it's the only car she's ever owned. She would sell her arm first. People approach her on the street to buy it. "I just laugh at 'em." Her father bought it for her when she was in college. "My husband always tried to sell this car. He'd offer me Opels and Camaros; I said no. Cause I really loved the car." For what it's worth, she still has the car, but no longer has the husband. Gail is a blonde, good-looking, young California-girl type, and she has one of the great good-time self-display cars ever made. As a singles car, she says it's "perfect." It features the 289 engine and automatic stick and is close to mint. Her father ran the same engine in a pickup for over 150,000 miles. She takes it in for a major tune once a year whether needed or not; sometimes the mechanic just dusts it. She drives it up to the snow on regular skiing trips and says it's impervious to the cold. She runs it on regular. Sigh.

NOTE THE RARE LEATHER rumble seat. Note the rare non-Ford Kelsey/Hayes wheels, the two accessory side-mirrors, the Greyhound hood ornament, the banjo steering wheel, and the rear-view mirror with built-in clock. Owner Dick Hanson is infected with Accessory-Fever. This was a candy-apple-everything hotrod when he got it. He paid $2100 up front, laboriously restandardized it about $1000 worth, and now has something worth ten or twenty grand, depending. It is totally self-restored; he made the front windshield-frame himself, an exact duplicate of the original. When you can't find a part, *make* it. All of this took years, however. "I've changed everything but the paint," he phews. One thing unaltered, however, is the .38 bullet hole just behind the left headlight. One of the car's former owners was killed in the so-called "Victor Massacre," just outside of Lodi, California some years back. There is also a crack in the windshield, "right about where the driver sits," Hanson grins. In most cases, however, this model was a sporty, semi-luxury *pleasure* car; and one of the most expensive open cars for its day—$625, a lot of dough during the Depression. Hanson isn't a mechanic and insists that such a total restoration is a simple matter of "taking the bull by the horns." This is a common way of getting gored, however; and hats off to Hanson. Note the *very* rare luggage rack, which came off a farm tractor in Livermore, where it was in service as a step-stool.

THIS WAS VARIOUSLY KNOWN as the Edsel of convertibles, the first semi-convertible, and a blend of car and erector set. There would be many attempts to produce a hardtop based on convertible styling and lines—the 1965 Mustang was the height of this approach—but the Skyliner tried it using an actual hard top which retracted automatically, in its entirety, into the trunk. It was a marvel of automotive schizophrenia and represents the ultimate thrust of technology to have both an open and closed car simultaneously, a contradiction in terms *and* economics. This exercise lasted only from 1957–59, and only 48,394 came off the line. The top involved seven motors, 20 relays and switches, and 200 yards of wiring. A certified milestone car, it was never duplicated, and perhaps just as well. More than a noble attempt to crossbreed hard and soft tops, it was the closest thing to an aircraft carrier ever put on wheels. A great broad swath of a car, its very bulk made the idea of a cloth top somehow self-defeating and inappropriate—like wearing a beanie with a tuxedo. Though it never really caught on with collectors, it is sustained by a small, rabid following. Skyliners are still occasionally available for under $2000, but are clearly a car for obsessives. The raise/lower operation was guaranteed to draw a crowd, even if something went wrong—*especially* if something went wrong—but the top was cumbersome and consumed the entire trunk. Says one collector simply, "It was a nightmare."

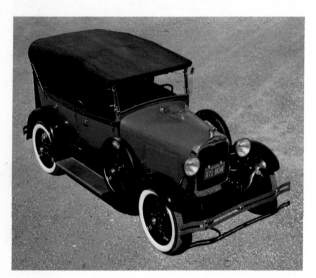

Here you have an historical event—one of the first affordable family-car convertibles. The Model T had been around for years, but was thoroughly rudimentary, with a bare-minimum engine which did little more than run and a basic two-speed trans. By contrast, the Model A offered nearly 40 horsepower and a conventional 3-speed, and was the first mass-produced car on an engineering par with previous, more limited-edition lines. While powerful, its four-cylinder engine was as simple as any ever made, and it sold in the neighborhood of $400. Comparatively speaking, this was lunch money, and the family convert was suddenly liberated from an exclusive automotive banquet. It's a milestone car but not a classic—the difference being whatever the Classic Car Club of America says it is, usually a matter of production and quality. Charles Goodman found this one unrestored at 16,000 miles, put in a new engine and did some bodywork, and replaced the interior which was gutted. It's anything but original—vinyl top, not canvas; and naugehyde seats, not leather. Neither is it particularly unique—there are maybe thousands of these around, spread over many model years. But it was the car that brought Ford back into parity with Dodge and Chevy, and this one still serves for regular short runs.

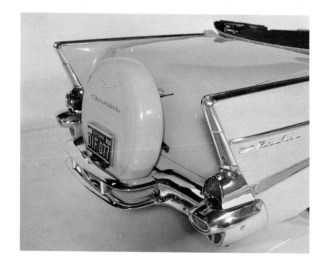

IN 1955, CHEVY MERGED its early '50s rounded lines with the Ford strongbox look and came up with this. One of the most immensely popular American cars ever, the Bel Air was the mobile icon of youth for ten years. When new, it was an affluence car, but it was as a *used* car that it endured for a decade in persistently large numbers on the highways. With Chevy's first V-8 power unit, it was GM's definitive attempt to create a factory-built, all-purpose hotrod. It was considered perfection in design, and adolescents saved money for years for one. Bel Airs lent themselves marvelously to alteration and power-beefing, and with them customizing and street-racing came of age. It also became the first great *cruising* car. Like the Mustang and VW, it defied obsolescence long after production ceased. The classic youthmobile, it went like a thief in the night and was *the* car to own among the Happy Days generation. Although all were hot, the 1955–57 years were the apex, and now unique, since Chevy totally abandoned the design in 1958. The '57 is the rarest and a one-time-only design shot featuring a continental kit and Chevy's only vertical tailfins; a transition car. "If you were going to *order* a collector's car, this would be it," says owner Owens. His is almost mint, with power brakes/windows and the anodized gold grille. You might have gotten an identical car in 1963 for $900, and plenty of low-riders did, driving them rapidly to death. As a result, it was one of the first big appreciators in the current clothtop boom, and if you can get one today for $4000, you're stealing it. This one has 29,000 miles, and Owens gets letters from all over offering to buy it.

THIS MOBILE SPECTACLE set records for design exaggeration, garish flamboyance, historical significance and impracticality—not to mention size. The body extended eight feet beyond the wheelbase, and the whole thing was a hair short of 23 feet long. But with all this enormity, the rear-seat legroom was adequate only if you were a pygmy. You could commit hara-kiri by throwing yourself on the fins, which were the ultimate expression of 11 years of tailfin-mania, physical growth and designer-excess. "Horrendous," shudders one collector. It was the gaudiest car of the post-war era and was made for only two years. But like most Cadillacs, it was well-built and a marvelously snotty and conspicuous self-indulgence. Paul Newman drove a 1957 Biarritz model in *Hud*. It was probably the first great factory-built pimpmobile—flagrantly exorbitant and lascivious—and the last successful blend of sexiness and luxury in a convertible. The *Jaws*-like fins jutted from a sleeky tapering rounded rear, and some consider the lines already classic. The '59 was noted for its handling, and some El Dorado engines got up around the 500 horsepower range, a formidable combination of raw power and mechanical excellence. This one is owned by Frank DeGrasse, who *never* puts the top up, and whose wife is said to despise it.

Believe it or not, this Duesenberg-built, Buehrig-designed marvel was a "dirt-cheap" car when new. Practically chrome-free and unlined by trim, it was Auburn's attempt to corner some of the 1930's cheap-car dollar—built and priced to compete with Ford at less than $1000, peanuts at the time. The chassis ran from a snub-nosed radiator to a single prow in the rear, looking rather like a dolphin with a nose job or an upside-down canoe with wheels. Its lines haven't really been duplicated before or since, and later Auburn Boattails grew far larger and bulkier. This, the two-seat sport model, was never made in great quantity and is rare to the degree of $40,000. It has *two* floor shifts—one just for overdrive—and like the Cord features the "suicide" door with the hinge in the rear and the latch and handle at the front, opening so as to catch the wind or anything else unlucky enough to pass too close to it. The hideaway top folded into a hatch-covered compartment, the Winged Victory hood ornament was flanked by two enormous chrome headlamps, and the two rear stoplights actually said STOP when lit. As classically distinctive a car as was ever mass-produced.

ONE OF THE CLASSIC "woody" designs held over from pre-World War II, the T&C's flawless straight-8 engine and Fluid-Drive semi-automatic trans made it a veritable indulgence to drive. Bruce Sorel got this one via word-of-mouth from the second owner. It floors collectors everywhere. More a thing of beauty, comfort and smooth riding than a historical milestone, it still screams with rarity—only 22 are known of, ranging from mint level to parts cars. This was a mess when bought in 1972 for $900. A professional mechanic, Sorel added $1100 worth of parts (at discount rates) and six months of labor, which works out to another $7000. He figures it's worth about ten thou, but "I couldn't care less if the market fell on its nose tomorrow." This one's a keeper. It had one of the early hydraulic tops, which is still reliable. The wood exterior, which simply stuns the eye, was restored by a woodworker; it reflects a level of resurrection which demands exacting cabinetwork skill and staggering patience. He says, "If the owner can't do the work himself, I'd tell him to forget it." He's a self-confessed Chrysler nut—"The family always had 'em, and they were always good cars"—and a collector, not an investor. It's strictly an occasional, warm-weather, pure-exuberance car, driven only "when the sun shines and the mood hits me." He starts it up once a month to charge the battery, wouldn't use it for straight transportation even under physical threat, and *never* allows it to get wet. "It's never been washed. In the winter it goes into hibernation." With 64,000 miles on it, it still gets 17 mpg on the highway. Not too shabby, for art.

[Catalog continued on page 105]

[YOU ARE WHAT YOU DRIVE.]

"I OWNED A CONVERTIBLE ONCE."

Five rare words, which mean that you once probably endured a mechanical ordeal and bared your soul to the grimmer elements and highway fumes; but they also say that you once were something *special*, which outweigheth an ark of deficiencies. Say those five words and nobody will go "tsk tsk." But someone, assuredly, will answer, "Hey, so did I, once. . . ."

Phrases like "the magic of the convertible" are wistful inaccuracies. Actually, it had no magic. What it had was a distinct expression of personality and the ability to nourish fantasies. It was magic only in the sense that it created illusion. It made the driver appear to be things he or she not always was: sexy, single, successful, stylish, spirited. That power in itself is magic to a lot of people.

The convertible's "mystique" derived not from what it was, but from what it represented. The open car rang with a note of unrestrained self-indulgence, was likened unto sculpture and other fine art, was called the classic expression of glorious excess. The convertible's story is more a matter of character than mechanics. Beyond mere transportation, it was an *attitude* toward transportation. Nothing conveyed the "racing car effect" so well short of actual racing, or the feel of speeding outside of really doing so, which presented hazards like $50 fines and manslaughter arraignments. Ragtops aroused the latent hedonism and unrequited mad streaks in us all.

They were fatalistic cars, implicit statements that nobody lives forever, so why not maximize the time devoted to irresponsibility? They expressed a cheeky arrogance, a refusal to grow up or to face reality. Such phrases as "breezing along" with your "head in the clouds" in weather so clear that "the sky's the limit" were all basic ragtop slang and utterly meaningless in a closed car.

The "magic" of convertibles lies in the fact that each one is special and almost every one distinct, and this condition can only accelerate from now on, given the inverse relationship between availability and conspicuousness. Bizi-Bodis and Econovans like murals may stand out on the highway right now, but we'll see how striking they are when there are 14,000,000 of them on the road. Everyone, however, reacts to the ragtop—from rednecks who grimace with raw envy to intellectuals who stew in their Volvos with jealous rectitude. The convertible has always been an icon of irreverence, from the Flaming Youth era right up to the 1950's, when it was beloved by the Beat subculture for its jazzbo insolence and audacious funkiness. It remains true for every generation that an adolescence without access to a ragtop was somehow deficient.

Let's not forget the purely tangible enjoyments of driving a ragtop. It is unquestionably the best thing on four wheels for moving about on warm, clear days; absolutely the car-of-choice for the beach. It delivers the sun like nothing else, washes you with warm air and is cheaper and more ecological than car air-conditioning which also ransacks your sinuses. It is matchlessly convenient at drive-in banks/movies/eateries. In the sense that it removes barriers between you and nature, it is *natural*. Conservatives can bask in the knowledge that they're driving an American tradition, and Liberals can look down their noses at wasteful spendthrifts in new economy imports, secure in the knowledge that *they* are *recycling*.

On a winding rural road in nice weather the open car provides the freedom of movement and racing exhilaration of skiing, surfing and skateboarding. The effect is basically the same: slinging oneself through the environment. Automotively, it's as close as we can come to riding on air. Driving in the open air conveys a feeling of movement, velocity and unfettered liberation which is destroyed by walls, even those with safety-glass windows.

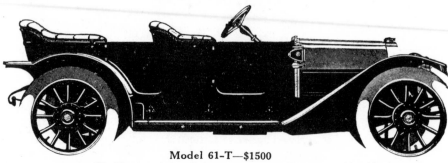

The Willys-Overland Company, Toledo, Ohio

Model 61-T—$1500

Wheel base, 115 inches; body, 5-passenger, touring; motor, 4⅜ x 4½; horse-power, 45; Bosch magneto; tires, 34 x 4 inch Q. D.; finish, Brewster green, ivory stripe, all bright parts nickel plated. Price, $1500.

THE CONVERTIBLE'S DECLINE was the end of a love affair only in the puppy-love sense. We did a terrible thing to the ragtop—we outgrew it. Its death is easily ascribed to such assassins as air-conditioning, pollution, safety-consciousness and vandalism, but what really doomed it was our own changing view of the world. The hardtop driver was practical, conservative, serious, settled, dignified and reclusive. The convertible driver was whimsical, experimental, foolish, impetuous, showy and extroverted. We are defined by the life we lead, and as we did an increasing amount of our living in cars, the cars we drove reflected where we were gravitating as a society. Once upon a time we were convertible people; now we're not. That is the bottom line on the convertible's epitaph.

Americans have been called comfort junkies, but this is a universal human addiction; we've just been able to indulge it to unprecedented degrees in this country. There's plenty to be said for comfort. It beats hell out of misery and deprivation; almost anyone would choose it over irritation and inconvenience. But comfort is fundamentally passive—in contrast to discomfort, which is stimulating and challenging. Riding with the top down represented fearlessness, intrepidation, the absence of fear or annoyance amid the environment. There was no felt need or desire to cloister the self within an assembly-line porta-womb which protected and concealed one from an implicitly hostile, nosy or perturbing outside world. You didn't go through the world in a convertible; you

were part of the world.

The difference between being exposed and being insulated is the difference between freedom and restriction. If there was ever a society which made its own rolling prisons and chrome-gilded cages, it's ours, which cultivates the premise that security and anonymity are more important and gratifying than openness and dash. The growing emphasis on making cars safer, buttressing the walls between ourselves and an essentially unpleasant and hazardous world, indicates that we've lost considerable trust and confidence in others, and ourselves. We no longer race through the wind. We buckle ourselves in. That the convertible represents optimism and the sedan a sort of pessimism is pervasively clear.

Lest we go overboard, we hasten to add that anything can be a vehicle for pop sociology, but that's no reason to go on a pointless spree of relating all American neuroses to the decline of the ragtop. We're just talking about transportational machinery here, which only goes so far as a fulcrum for social analysis. America's shift from rag to metal tops symbolizes both growth and diminution, progress and regression. It's a basic truth that frivolity is the price of maturity. The childish joy of the open car isn't the first we've sacrificed to pragmatism, and it won't be the last. The question of pleasure versus rationality doesn't pivot on it, but it's not a bad metaphor for a much larger social process which is from a sense of community to one of individuality and isolation.

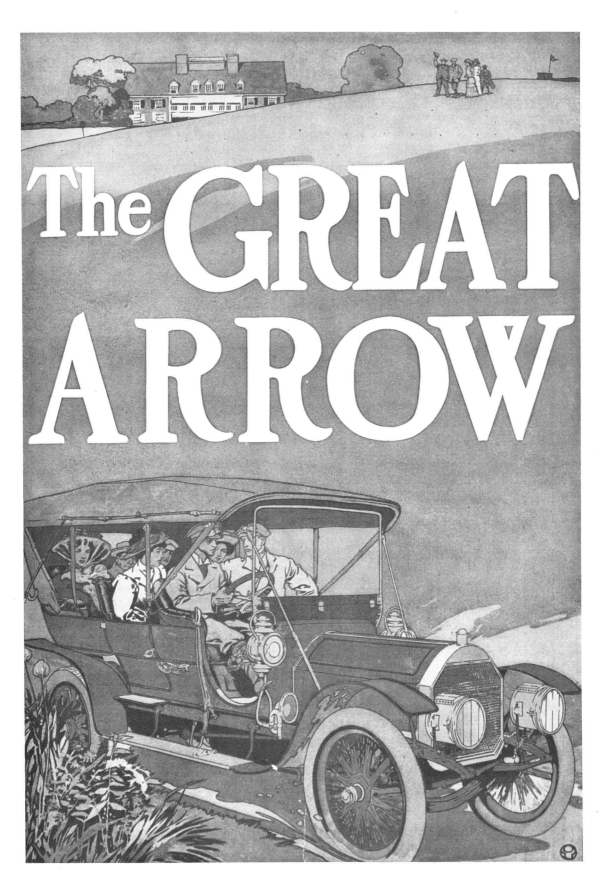

The GREAT ARROW

A NEW MOTOR-CAR WITH A NEW CHAUFFEUR

THE PSYCHOLOGICAL VIRTUES of the convertible are so tempting that it's easy to overlook the hard-headed mechanical issues involved. Beset by praise of European engineering and wild advertising claims, we tend to forget that cars built ten years ago in America didn't exactly fall apart at the touch. Some of the best cars on the road are five to ten years old with 25,000–60,000 miles on them; the average American car of this vintage will go 100,000 miles before any major breakdown. According to *Automobile Facts & Figures*, over half the cars sold in 1964 were still going strong in 1974. The fact that so many are still on the highways indicates they weren't put together haphazardly, and some '60s units are among the most solidly-built automobiles ever to come out of Detroit. Some collectors consider a good used car nothing less than a new car with calluses.

Naturally, a used-car won't give you new-car durability or performance; but mechanically, it has many arguments going for it. Engines of the '60s were built like dams—before emissions-control devices diminished mileage, performance and efficiency, and filled the roads with touchy experimental engines. They churned out vast horsepowers at relatively few rpm's and low temperatures. They stayed obediently in tune for 10,000 miles and more. They were less complex and temperamental; routine maintenance actually *was* routine. If you were smart enough to keep up the payments, you were smart enough to keep up the car. People commonly got 100,000 miles out of these plants, and if decay and/or disaster ever befell the engine, you could—and still can—have it completely rebuilt from the short block on up for about $600 in 1977 money. The result is usually worth another 100,000 miles.

A big benefit of low-maintenance-era cars is that unless the previous owner was accident-prone, a car with less than 85,000 miles on it can be kept running without great outpourings of sweat and currency. Generally, these cars can be expected to have taken some shots in traffic and may have seven or so years'

worth of wear and tear, but most convertibles were part of large-volume sedan or coupe lines whose entrails and components are still abundant. And used parts—a prime example of responsible recycling—happen to be one of the best remaining bargains in the auto industry. As to the top: eventually, any cloth roof will flop around and leak insulation and weather. But new tops are surprisingly available everywhere —for as little as $40. Try replacing a banged-up metal roof for that.

Certainly, there are points against the used ragtop, but none of them are sharp enough to pierce the benefits:

1) *They are old.* True, but only a few years beyond "old" lies that marvelously profitable category called "antique." When it comes to convertibles, older usually means better. And keep it in mind that most of the cars on the road are "old"—five years or more.

2) *They devour gas.* Some did, and some didn't. Most new recreation/pleasure vehicles devour as much or more—in the 9–15 mpg range. Many mid-'60s compacts got better mileage than most recent sizes. Mustangs, Skylarks and Malibus were good for 15–20 mpg; Corvairs and Falcons frequently got 20+; the VW rated 25–35 depending on the year; and even GTOs, Cougars and Firebirds topped 15 mpg. Only in a recent compact or subcompact will you do much better than that. By comparison, *Consumer Reports'* 1976 ratings pegged the Chevy Nova, Dodge Aspen and Ford Granada compacts at a city/highway average of 16 mpg, and most mid-size models at less than 15.

3) *They're unsafe.* No more so than the person at the wheel makes them, through heedless driving, careless maintenance or general indifference. Brakes, seat belts, lights and sobriety have far more to do with safety than tops.

Lest this sound like blind enthusiasm, it should be noted that ragtops and other classica are not for everybody, especially not for those interested in economy, trouble-free durability and buyer-security. Let's face it: the "logical arguments" for ragtop ownership are more rationalization than pure reason. The real motivation of any convertible owner isn't horse sense; it's hedonism. But cheer up. You-are-what-you-drive isn't a fixed law, and owning a Rabbit doesn't necessarily make you one, any more than owning a Cougar does, despite what the commercials insist.

Even as the experts were proclaiming the cloth top to be finished, it was in many ways just getting started. The more uniformity burgeoned in the 1960's, the more car buyers sought individuality in their vehicles, and virtual cults arose around low-volume or specialty cars. By 1970, ragtop clubs were flourising. There was also a growing appreciation of old cars *because* they were old. The "car collector" became a thriving breed.

Inflation began to occur faster than dilapidation, so that used things were suddenly as good a buy as new ones—often better. The car was a prime example. The average 1978 American new-car sticker price is almost $6500. By the time you tack on state/local taxes, shipping, registration and licensing, not to mention dealer prep and options, you are staring into a $7000 tunnel. New-car prices have shot so far out of reason that, for sheer functional economy, many used cars are better values than their showroom descendants. The classifieds teem with hand-me-downs which are in only slightly worse condition than current models, for about half the price. Even when repairs are needed, they're usually a bargain compared to instant new-car depreciation of $500 or more; and older cars cost less in terms of taxes, licensing fees and replacement of parts.

If you drive off in a new car for less than $4000, you must be using a gun. This means that probably not only you can't afford one, but that millions of other people probably can't either. This situation has created a used-car market of enormous proportions. As demand has grown, so has price structure, to the point where used cars not only maintain their value, but often increase it. Used convertibles do even better—in good condition, they will *probably* appreciate.

Consider the situation. Traditionally, a car was worth 75 per cent of its showroom price after a year, 50 per cent after two, 35 per cent after three, 20 per cent after five, skidding to $1–$200 by age eight, after which it began reviving as a collector's item. But as of 1977, appreciation was beginning after three or four years, something unheard of since World War II. Reasons for this are multiple: economy-conscious drivers hold onto their cars longer, thus cutting used-car supply. Skyscraping new-car prices draw *all* car prices upward. As fewer new cars are sold, fewer trade-ins enter the market. And so on.

The result has been unprecedented used-car appreciation. In 1974, used-car wholesale prices rose from an average $1000 to $1175 in 12 months—a 17.5 per cent gain—and this was just for hardtops. In 1977, some pony cars were getting $400–$500 over their bottom-out 1973 prices, and mid-'60s Mustangs were up almost $1000 from 1972. A 1967 Camaro 327 worth $925 in 1975 was worth $1600 two years later. 1971 Pintos haven't depreciated since 1974, and some cars—such as the Pontiac Trans Am—sell for close to their showroom figures. Other solid value-holders are Valiants, Darts and Novas.

The market for convertibles is bubbling even faster, and the combination of steadily-growing demand and no new supply-source is expected to raise it to a boil by 1980. *Sixty Minutes* filmed a segment on the clothtop phenomenon, and articles laden with nostalgic awe pop up regularly in the press. The word is out. Indeed, the smart money saw Detroit's phaseout coming and started buying in 1974. Since the last open Caddie in 1976, things have simply gone berserk.

With zero new American convertibles being built and attrition steadily working on those in existence, another model is delivered into rarity almost every month. Those in good shape are so hot you could weld with them, at such a premium that they rise in value almost without exception. The more their investment value is known, the more sought after they'll become, and the greater their value, *ad circulum*. The 1976 El Dorado had a sticker price of $12,000, but if you could get one from a dealer for under 20 grand, it was charity. The car was a collector's item while it was still on the drawing board, and GM had to double production to turn out 14,000 units to meet the last desperate rush of the rich and investment-minded. The moment you signed the papers, you made ten per cent.

Students of these matters estimate that a used car's value is enhanced as follows: air conditioning—$200; deluxe "image" decor package—$200; sunroof—$100. This adds up to $500, a figure which decreases with age and wear. By comparison, a lowerable top boosts a car's value by at least 20 per cent. At a $2500 base, this also comes out to $500. Since it's a function of design, not performance, this figure will tend to rise with time. The *Blue Book* appraises tagtops at an average $300 over solid tops, and people in the business appraise them at $400–$500 over that.

THERE WAS REAL ENTHUSIASM OVER THEIR NEW BATHTUB
MODEL WHEN THEY REACHED COUNTRY ROADS

Before the Plunge Takes You.⟧

Few qualities are more desirable and hard to come by than uniqueness, a commodity the convertible is now blessed with. GM, for all its corporate might, day-glo vans and player's cars, can't provide a simple ragtop. It is an image goldmine whose vanity-potential runs in megavolts. Since a convertible can now only be bought from an owner, the owner has considerable say regarding its worth. In this context, a 1955 T-Bird is better than the deed to the ranch. Even early '70s convertibles are becoming collector's items; people are already buying some models and stashing them. Experts figure *any* decently-maintained ragtop will appreciate 10–20 per cent a year, which is better than land. And, notes one aficionado, "You can't have fun driving land."

Most states classify cars 25 years or older as "antiques." But convertibles achieve this status unofficially five to ten years earlier, hence you only have to go back to 1960's models to find a collector's item. Unfortunately, you'll often find a collector there first, checkbook in hand, and unless you can compete financially on the connoisseur level, your market is confined to nice, hold-their-own transportation cars with cloth tops and solid resale value.

You can still get a serviceable open car of 1965–72 vintage for $500 to $2500—not only a good price for automotive transportation, but an almost unthinkable buy in terms of rarity. Given the inevitable collapse and/or destruction of a certain number of con-

vertibles each year, and the fact that nobody *makes* the damn things any more, you wind up with a truly remarkable bargain-basement investment.

Late-model convertibles aren't classics, mind you; just anachronisms. If they qualify as art, fine, but we're concerned with operable vehicles, to be driven on the streets like favorite shoes are worn—lovingly, regularly and for as long as possible. These cars can be restored to near-mint status or simply left alone as funky *character* cars. Either way, you'll probably make money on one when you finally turn it over to someone else with The Craving. Barring a major economic collapse—in which case *no* investment is secure—the American convertible can only appreciate and diminish, and appreciate and diminish. This is basically the formula behind the financial success of Big Oil.

In a nutshell: You can still buy a solid, attractive convertible for under $2500, provided you exercise the prudence and judgment involved in buying any used car. You can reasonably expect several years of enjoyable driving at less cost-per-mile than many newer American cars offer and have an excellent chance of selling it for more than you put into it. As more people discover this phenomenon, it will become not a matter of whether, but of how quickly to buy. "You can't lose on it," grins one collector. "What other investment can you drive to work?"

Vol. 61, No. 1576
Copyright, 1913, Life Publishing Company

Life

PRICE 10 CENTS
January 9, 1913

The Self Propelled Vehicle Number

T HE REST OF THIS SECTION is largely how-to information. If you're seriously thinking of obtaining a ragtop, you should read through it. If you're just mildly curious about the rules of the game, here is a Shopper's Synopsis:

In general, try for a car being sold by the original owner. This boosts value considerably and usually signifies good maintenance. Stick with cars which are solid, reasonably cared-for, and with no signs of accident damage. Once you've bought one, do whatever is necessary to put it in top shape, including a paint job and rebuilt engine; you'll get your money back at resale time. And do this promptly, since repair costs will be going up. Then *maintain* the car properly; it will run far more economically, far longer.

Buyer-wisdom, informed scrutiny and simple common sense can lower your rip-off risk-factor by a healthy margin, but don't kill yourself trying to find the perfect car. There is no such animal. Perhaps the best suggestion is to buy whatever steals your heart and hope for the best. If you want to put your money on something stronger than hope, however, you're advised to digest the following Rules to Buy by:

If Wishes Were Autos

HOW MUCH IS TOO MUCH can only be assessed in terms of the day-to-day market, which is out of the province of this and most other publications. "As little as you can get away with" isn't a frivolous answer, but a sensible guideline, given cost-estimating formulae which are vague at best. Your local bank or savings-and-loan can provide the latest monthly *National Automobile Dealers' Association Official Used Car Guide*, which lists the wholesale and retail prices of all models. Expect to pay at least the retail amount when buying from a dealer or middleman, and presume that any prices shown for ragtops are $100–$500 out of date at any given time.

The used convertible market has become so volatile that most price-lists are obsolete by the time they're printed. The *Kelly Blue Book* undervalues almost every one by an indecent amount—at least $250—but when dealing with a naive or unaware private party, its authority may nail down a deal several hundred bucks below real value in hand-to-hand bargaining. The classifieds and local swap meets are better indicators of going rates. If you can't find your desired ragtop listed for sale, take the average price of the car's hardtop model and add 15–25 per cent.

Hit several new-car dealers who sell the brand you have in mind and go straight-talk the used-car manager. Tell him what you're looking for, what your cash structure is, and ask him how the market looks. When he stops laughing, he'll probably have nothing even close to what you want, but this may incline him more toward blunt honesty than sales hype. Ask around; develop a working consensus.

If you have an actual car test-driven and tugging at your wallet, ask the mechanic you've taken it to what he would pay for the car. This is your practical limit beyond which you have to put your own price on your own passion. Also get any mechanic's estimate of likely repair costs and use this as markdown-leverage when bargaining. Above all, don't let anyone sales-talk you except yourself.

By and large, alas, you get what you pay for and pay for what you get. Those who've kept close watch on their ragtop will usually have kept close watch on its value, and will charge accordingly; but in terms of buyer-security, they're your best bet for a good, dependable car. If you have a particular year and/or model in mind, of course, you vastly increase the chances of having to take whatever you can get in the way of working condition and price.

In most cases, there is some latitude for horse-trading in used-car buying, but the ragtop isn't most cases, and this is not exactly a buyer's market. Unless you're dealing with a naive owner, really know whereof you speak; or unless the car is clearly overpriced, don't get cute. Getting cute with the knowledgeable dealer or buff is even less advisable—as often as not, he'll tell you to take your checkbook and cute remarks elsewhere.

Moreover, try not to get carried away and grow so anxious to grab your particular dream car that you end up with a nightmare. Overeagerness has cost more people more money than heroin. Don't be so struck by the sudden perfect combination of color, model and style that you overlook such pithy realities as Does The Sucker Run? Keep in mind your goal— a used car that's nearly as good as new and several grand cheaper. The bedrock secret of this trade is *patience*, in great quantities, followed by swift and decisive action on the order of a hungry panther. Don't be rushed by the seller; if it's such a chance-of-a-lifetime, why's it still wearing a For Sale sign? Indeed, why is it being sold? Haste makes regret. Wait, wait, wait for the *right* car; visually, spiritually and mechanically—and once all the criteria have been absolutely verified, pounce.

Try to pounce with cash in hand, however, since unless you have a love affair with a local bank, you'll never get a loan for a pre-'70s car from legitimate sources. Paying cash also saves same—dealer and finance-company loans will bleed you white; banks aren't much better. Cash money can also tip a wavering owner over the Sell line and close a deal before he or she has time to reconsider. As a rule, try to accumulate the dough while you're researching the car in question and the local market lay-of-the-land.

This is the Cole "50" Electric Starting Touring Car

$1985

Remember when you bought your first motor car—the wise front you put up when the salesman began jabbering about the "carburetor" and the "differential"?

FIRST, DECIDE WHAT you're looking for in a car—size, economy, splash, handling—bearing in mind how you'll use it, the cost and availability of parts and servicing, and the fact that make, year and model-reputation aren't as important as a particular car's actual condition.

Barring any sudden, stupefying bargains, wintertime is the time to buy—clothtop owners are less able to extol their cars' virtues, and may even be impatient with them due to the weather; also, there are fewer buyers amid the second-thoughts of icy temperatures. New car trade-ins swell the used-car supply, making December the slowest month in the business, and prices slump accordingly. And although a basic car buyer's maxim is Don't Buy in The Rain—dents and scapes are less evident, and cars sound and feel better and more solid against an inclement backdrop—at least one wet-weather test-drive is vital in the case of a car with a cloth top.

Where to buy depends on how much you know about cars and how much you're willing to pay. The safest place to buy any used car, ironically, is from a new car dealer, who is bound by all manner of regulations and will stand to suffer the most by deceiving

you. Lawsuits and bad reputations are arsenic to a major dealership, and many of these, since they have to upgrade what they sell anyway, will throw in a guarantee. And new-car dealers will have the pick of each new trade-in crop. In general, stick with dealers you know, or who come personally recommended, or who sell the line of car you're looking for, in that order. Since they rely on steady clientele and repeat sales, they're more likely to have serviced—and kept records on—the stock in their used-car inventory. You may just want to stake out several franchises dealing in your desired line and wait to see what pops up. Don't expect to find too many this way, though. Convertibles are more cult-market than trade-in material, and even if a dealer gets one, he'll probably hold onto it or sell it at collector-car value, in which case it may be no bargain.

In all likelihood, you'll wind up talking business with a used-car dealer or an unfamiliar private party, which are more or less tied for second in desirability. Their shared drawback is Unknown Reliability, and here you are left to your own wits, but these aren't bad odds if you know what to look (and look out) for—which you will, if you finish this section.

New **SUPER-CHARGED** *Models*

You Would Not Trust with Your Daughter.⟧

Used-car dealers, who rank in public esteem somewhere between Congressmen and pushers, have service capacities ranging from limited to none, which usually makes warranties out of the question. They tend to get new-car dealers' castoffs or third-owner jobs, meaning any convertibles they pick up will be probably be in weak shape. "Jewels" are almost unheard of. Try to concentrate on long-time dealers with solid local reputations. The Better Business Bureau reports complaints filed against local dealers and the settlement of same, if any. "Unanswered complaints" are the *nolo contenderes* of auto sales, and not good. Flee the cities—smaller, outlying-area lots must move cars faster to maintain cash flow and can't command the prices of high-volume lots, and they seem to get proportionately more and better open cars. Says one pro: "The average guy is simply out of luck in finding a collector car at a reasonable price unless he hits the boondocks."

The small, tidy, independent lot is best. Try to deal with the lot owner, not a salesman on commission, and compare prices with similar items in the paper and at new-car agencies. Ignore warranties. Even those on new cars are more sales ploy than reflection of the car's mechanical state. In the case of something with 35,000–50,000 miles and several years, guarantees are purely a matter of personal faith and shouldn't influence your judgment. What's important is dealer reputation. Most locales require by law that used cars be sold only in safe driving condition. Those are the locales for you. Remember that cars tend to look better in freshly-washed rows than on the street. Sign nothing, and don't leave any deposit with a dealer or salesman during a test-run or inspection check. Stay alert. "Used-car salesman" is widely considered a synonym for "crook," and this is not by accident.

I F DEALING WITH used-car outfits is a lot like dealing with the Arabs, dealing with individuals, especially where ragtops are involved, is not usually much better, and you're crazy to go in uninformed. Private parties aren't always so private. When answering a classified, ask first if the seller is in fact a dealer. If so, and the ad didn't mention this, bail out. Omission of the facts is something you don't need. Many "private parties" are basically closet car-middlemen who may sell half a dozen a year and frequently specialize in locating tasty vintage autos with strong widespread followings and selling them at appropriate markups. You may be dealing with a semi-pro. When in doubt, ask, and if it turns out that you're at a "driveway agency," get a few names of previous buyers to contact for references. If none are produced and you're not a seasoned judge of car-flesh, take your dough elsewhere.

Keep it in mind that even original-owner cars can be disasters as great as anything from a fly-by-night agency. Why, in fact, is the owner selling this gem? Since buyer and seller are eliminating the middle-man's cut, this is where the bargains usually are, but not where warranties, legal recourse or time-payments are. The FTC recently estimated that for every used car sold by a new- or used-car dealership, three more are sold in private-party deals. There is greater control on the Mafia than over these millions of private transactions, and more people get burned in this market than in kitchen fires. Federal regulations require any seller to sign an odometer-accuracy affidavit, but this requirement means little and goes largely ignored. The one-on-one deal can be the best kind, but only as long as you (1) know and can trust the owner/seller, or (2) are provided extensive repair and maintenance records along with the merchandise. The best buy is a car that's been in the family or neighborhood.

Even these items can prove catastrophic, though, especially to the relationship between buyer and seller, and should be approached cautiously. Persons otherwise stiff with honesty and propriety are often seized with guile and deceit when it comes to selling their car. Nevertheless, the one-owner personal transportation or recreation convertible is your best shot, given a fair amount of comparison shopping and some homework on your part.

For instance, check out the seller as well as the car. The seller was the former user, and there is probably less wear on anything driven by a librarian than by a high school cheerleader. In many cases the ragtop will have been mainly a tool of excess and will suffer for it, but in just as many cases it will have been the well-kept-up and beloved weekend car, more cherished than driven. Try to look for persons who *loved* their ragtop rather than those who *used* it. Insurance actuarial tables suggest you be wary of the young, the low-income and the single. But a leather-covered punk with oilspill hair could indicate a car which was slavishly and knowledgeably maintained and attended to. Unfortunately, the more devoted the owner, the higher the price, in general.

Used cars sold by dealerships must pass at least some safety and reliability requirements in most states. Find out what your state requires, and use that information as your baseline in private-party deals. Don't settle for less than the government would. And read between the lines of the classifieds. Avoid ominous speculation items—"CHEV '65 Impala convt. needs work. $350/offer. 555-2345. Frenchie." Beware of deadly little understatements: "mechanic's special" amounts to little more than a curse, and "Looks good, runs," is probably wild praise. Follow up on a couple dozen classifieds to learn the ropes and terminology.

However don't put a lot of faith in the ads. Evermore, the choice converts are sold within the family, neighborhood or peer-group. Many of the super-deals described in the catalog section were obtained either this way or circumstantially—via divorce, or from the army-bound or in trade for a camper. The golden buys seldom see the light of print or car lot. There's also the ragtop collector's grapevine to contend with, but this applies mostly to older/rarer items; a good argument for post-1968 or less popular cars. Despite all this, each day brings a few convertibles whose owners have knuckled under to the energy crisis, or acquired sudden debt, or whatever. An outstanding ragtop buy will almost certainly be more a matter of luck—being in the right place at the right time—than the result of methodical shopping.

Auto swap meets can be excellent sources of convertibles, ranging from total classic restorations to decent used transport cars. One collector recommends swap meets "because you can dicker with the owners. There are no dealers involved, and they'll often have stickers showing the price or best offer. By the end of the day, you can usually make a very good deal. But some cars are heavily over-priced, and the person who doesn't really know should tread with caution. Take a friend who knows what he's doing, hopefully a mechanic."

Lists of swap meets are printed monthly in *Hemming's Motor News* and other auto publications and are usually announced in the Automotive or Collector's column in the classifieds. At many meets, mimeographed lists of future meets are handed out. Meets are also a great parts source. But be warned that these gatherings will be heavy with full-restoration class cars carrying hefty price tags. Tales are told of 1955 Bel Airs from non-collectors at basement rates, but far more are told of versions at $4000 a shot.

Auto auctions are similar but more hazardous. Persons out to make a killing flock here, spiff the car's exterior to mint-condition status, and put it on the block as such. In most cases test-drives and mechanical inspections are impossible, and you can't tell cosmetic hype from showroom material. Auctions also help drive used ragtop prices out of sight and are broadly scorned by the experts.

Auctions and meets are good places to meet collectors, however, and this crowd is constantly in touch with the best items available on the market. Get to know a couple; they may run into a choice deal that's not to their taste which they'll pass on to you in return for similar hot tips. And watch the papers for estate sales; these frequently include meticulously-kept older cars, and the heirs will often appraise and sell them cut-rate to lower their tax liability.

Some collectors ignore the market altogether and seek out their desired car on the streets and in driveways, then quietly let the owners know that if they should ever have a mind to sell, a buyer is ready. *Cash* buyers do best at this practice. You may want to stake out the car(s) of your choice and try this waiting-game tack. The note-under-the-wiper ploy will get no response 80 per cent of the time, but any reply rate in this market is good news.

When all else fails, there is the rash act known as California, which contains within its borders far and away more convertibles than any other state—anywhere from 50–85 per cent of those on the road. West coast cars are also virtually rust-free, and for ragtop worshippers, the California coast is Mecca. But these and other factors have sent prices soaring out West. In April of 1977, 1965 open Mustangs were listed in the San Francisco *Chronicle* for $1750–$2400; in the Cincinnati *Enquirer* for $600–$900. Even with Golden State ragtops' improved selection and decreased corrosion, this is some markup.

PACKARD

THE new Packard Twin Six develops more than 160 horsepower. Seldom, if ever, is it necessary to draw fully on such vast potential power—but the extra power is *there* and its advantages are constantly reflected in the matchless, smooth performance of this great, brand new Super-Packard. ¶ Speed greater than you will ever need is at your quick command—speed that is never labored, speed that always leaves something in reserve. Acceleration is as velvety and noiseless as a summer breeze. There has never been a car, we believe, so swift, so smooth, so silent. ¶ And how easily the Twin Six handles! Steering is almost effortless. Gears shift without a click.

Automatic clutch control, available at the flick of a finger, does away with constant clutch pedal operation and provides free-wheeling results. Brakes, with vacuum assist, operate with the gentlest of foot pressure. ¶ Those who have driven the new Packard Twin Six have freely pronounced it *America's finest car.* They base their judgment not only on its brilliant performance but on its majestic beauty, its distinguished luxury, its complete and restful riding ease. Discriminating opinion, wherever the car is known, agrees that today's Twin Six obsoletes all Vee-type cars of earlier engineering development. ¶ You are cordially invited to inspect and drive Packard's newest and greatest car.

— of a Distinguished family

PACKARD TWIN-SIX

Without a Scorecard. ⟧

THE LAW REQUIRES all car sellers to provide some written agreement as to their liability for false information, but many sellers will balk at this demand and pass on the deal. Even if they agree to it, collecting for a rip-off is costly and problematical, and intent to defraud or deceive must be proved. When buying from a dealer, try to get a disclosure statement listing the car's former owner, all signif-icant repair and maintenance work performed, and the specific terms of any warranty.

Beyond that, the final decision will be your own. Make it according to these basic carbuying check-points. The seller should allow you to make a com-plete mechanical inspection of the car without inter-ference or rushing. If he doesn't, back off.

☐ Maintenance. Ask to see all upkeep records, which should reveal periodic tune-ups, oil changes, lube jobs, air/gas filter replacements, cooling-system flush-es and wheel alignments. (Just *getting* these is a good sign; they mean the owner cared.)

☐ Body. Body repairs often cost more than engine repairs. Check fenders, doors, hood and trunk in full daylight for ripples, fresh paint and off-color sections. Such touch-ups may mean a major collision, which can lessen performance and longevity. Check all locks and jambs; loose or balky doors, trunk or hood give you an idea of how much use the car has seen.

☐ Front End. Frame damage here is especially com-mon, expensive and important in terms of perform-ance. Look between the radiator and grille for spot-welding or misalignment; former damage there is to be shunned.

☐ Engine. Encrusted sludge could mean engine damage, but don't overestimate cleanliness—steam-cleaned or spray-painted innards may tell you less than if they'd been left alone.

☐ Vital Parts. The battery should be corrosion-free. Check fan belts, ignition wires, spark plugs and the air cleaner for rust, gunk, cracks and flimsiness. Things held together by threads or friction tape mean a car that's suffered a life of cut corners.

☐ Controls. Do they all work? Test all lights, latches, switches, windows, seat adjustments, gauges, acces-sories and power options. Make sure hydraulic tops operate smoothly and latch easily in front.

☐ Rust. (The cancer of the car.) Inspect—by strong daylight—all exterior surfaces, under fenders, around tail pipes, beneath trunk floormats and under the chassis. Probe rust spots for weakness and decay—costly repairs. Common ragtop rust areas are the

moldings under and around the top, the joints and especially the top-storage area in the rear; use a flashlight. East coast cars are most rust-prone.

☐ Underside. Look for frame damage, missing bolts or bent underpinnings, which mean collision history. Doublecheck for rust; a heavy undercoating may cover corrosion.

☐ Leaks. Hunt for them around brakelines and cylinders, the engine, transmission, radiator, rear axle and gas tank.

☐ Chassis. Are the front suspension parts lubed? Push down briskly on each corner of the car; a slow or shaky return to normal means worn shocks.

☐ Tires. They should be the right size and load-range for the car as indicated in the owner's manual. Uneven tread-wear implies poor alignment, brakes or shock absorbers. Grab each one and shake it—rattling or looseness could be bad bearings or suspension. Recaps indicate a cheap driver, who may also have skimped on maintenance.

☐ Interior. Note signs of heavy usage and dilapidation—paint rubbed off surfaces, missing knobs or handles, shot seams, shredded seats, rips in headliner, cigarette burns throughout. (Remember—an active family can make upholstery look like the siege of Leningrad without affecting performance.)

☐ Mileage. Only a general indicator, but the closest thing to a numerical gauge of the car's use. It should average out to 10,000 a year. Distrust cars showing remarkably few miles for their age; check other parts (gas pedal, driver's seat, floormat) for equal wear. Recaps or brand new tires on a "20,000 mile car" are suspicious.

☐ Locale. Power trains wear faster in cities, and errand/commute miles are more taxing than long-haul miles. Find out where the car's been driven.

☐ Loving Touches. Has the owner devoted some time and money to upkeep or let it go to seed? Little things mean a lot when several don't work. Owner-maintained cars are often the best-maintained.

☐ Top. Is it frayed, ripped, brittle or stained? Is the rear window cracked or coming unsealed? Check all seals for decay and leaks. This is the interior's overhead protection and the car's most exposed working part. If *it's* been neglected, what hasn't?

☐ Ragtop Details. Some power windows seal poorly; run the car through a car wash. Some vinyl boot covers are known to shrink from cold or disuse and can be incredibly stubborn; remove it, work the top, replace it.

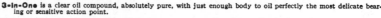
If THERE'S A Golden Rule in this game, it's this: *Drive* the damn thing! After all, that's what you're buying it for. And judge the car according to how you'll use it—on the freeway or stop-and-go, for regular family use or occasional tomfoolery, wide-open or gingerly. Statistically speaking, most lemon-buyers aren't taken, they hand themselves *over*; and the easiest way to do this is by not grabbing the wheel and putting the beast to a field test.

The car should start without difficulty or unnerving noise, and when given the juice, should under *no* conditions pour forth bluish-black smoke. Nor should there be sounds of tapping, knocking or coughing from beneath the hood. Listen closely. If the engine starts nicely but tends to misfire once warm or when run at high rpm's, you may need a new coil.

If you haven't already, now's a handy time to try everything—all the lights (head, tail, side, brake, fog, backup, warning and interior) as well as the radio, heater and anything electrically operated, especially the top. It should be fairly uncomplicated and quick to lower and even quicker to raise and lock in place.

Then run it. The car should accelerate and decelerate smoothly, with a uniform sound unbroken by noises. Get on the freeway and floor it, then look in the rearview mirror, first for the state police, then for exhaust smoke. The blue variety merely indicates carburetor work. The black version represents heavy overhaul costs. Accelerate and decelerate sharply and feel and listen for looseness in the rear end. With the car in gear, coast downhill. Backfire, popping or jerkiness is evidence of a chronically untuned car.

Get on some rocky, unpaved excuse for a road and put the hammer down. Is the car reasonably controllable, or does it cover the terrain like a kangaroo? Steering and maneuverability shouldn't go amok. Listen for tortuous squeaks and chatter in the joints.

Ask about every clank, rattle and whine. Convertibles are more prone to routine rattles and squeaks; make allowances for this.

Keep an eye on the temperature gauge. The car shouldn't run hot or, at the end of your test run, produce hissing or billows of steam. Illnesses of the cooling system involve brutally costly operations.

Let go of the wheel on a flat open surface at about 25 mph. Veering means realignment is needed. Hit the brakes. The pedal should hold high and firm and should stop the car within reasonable yardage and without jerkiness, noise or wavering. If the brakes fade, pull or need pumping, major repairs loom ahead. When the car has stopped, hold your foot on the pedal for a minute; if it sinks to the floor you have a leak. If the car dips sharply when braking, or sways heavily on curves and lane-changes, you're riding a bad set of shocks. The steering wheel should make the car go where you want it to go without undue effort, stickiness or give. A lot of play means a lot of trouble.

Put the transmission through all its gear changes several times. On a manual, you want to avoid rattles and grabbing. The clutch action should be smooth and emphatic, with no struggle or confusion involved. If it pops out of gear or makes noise, look out. On an automatic, bad signs are shudders and jerks during gear changes, or engine-whine between shifts. Listen closely. Marked rises in pitch or slushy-feeling shifts mean work ahead. If you don't know what a slushy shift feels like, get someone to show you. There should be emphatic, feelable gear-changes, with no delay or lurch. This can get tricky, though. Sluggish shifts may mean major transmission trouble, or just minor adjustments of the clutch (manuals) or friction-band (automatics). A mechanic should be enlisted to determine the truth. But in either case, if you run across a "ghost"—one that clanks, moans or

Stevens-Duryea

"Nearly a Quarter-Century of Leadership"

The C-Six sets a new standard for the fine motor-car.

$4500 to $5950
Catalogue on request

Stevens-Duryea Company
Chicopee Falls Mass
"Pioneer Builders of American Sixes"

shrieks—get thee and thy money hence.

After driving the car, keep the engine running and take off the coil cap and watch for smoke. Where there's smoke, there are imminent repair bills, and this is an automatic abort. Turn the engine off and:

Check the oil dipstick. Skim-milkish film thereon means engine trouble. Thick gouts of oil thereon may mean 60- or 90-weight oil has been used to deaden the sounds of ailing rods. Water thereon means water in the oil, which means a cracked block, which means at least a major overhaul and probably a whole new engine. Run, don't walk, away. *Nothing* thereon means wretched non-maintenance and probably ditto.

Check the transmission fluid dipstick. Any burnt odor is the kiss of death, making rigorous wear a certainty and repair work likely. The fluid should be of a robust strawberry-syrup color and consistency, not sooty or flecked with metal. If the maintenance records fail to mention the trans several times, you may be looking at the used-car's Achilles' heel.

Check the master brake cylinder for fullness (good) and leakage (bad). Low fluid could mean leaks elsewhere or worn brake linings. When the engine has cooled, check the water in the radiator. Rust on any metal or speckled in the water is ugly news; oiliness on the water is to be gone away from.

If you're truly sincere and committed, do yourself a favor and take the car to a shop or diagnostic center and write a check to a mechanic for the following: inspection of brakes, balljoints, suspension, steering play, exhaust system; a car-wide hunt for leaks, prior damage to the frame or chassis, and faults in all major components—especially for front-end problems, which cost more than color TVs and often go undetected. A test-drive by the mechanic is even better, and the $20–$40 involved is the best investment you can make at this point, not to mention the best available guarantee. A compression test is the very blood-pressure of the engine, and even at $50 is money well spent. An electronic diagnostic series will cost a few bucks more, but if you're up in the $3000 market and getting serious, it's worth it.

If nothing else, at least hire a mechanic to tutor you in automotive pathfinding and buyership. You'll save more money in the long run than a tax accountant. And if the seller refuses to permit extensive mechanical inspection, forget it.

The Stearns-Knight Car--

The Choice of Men Who Choose From All the World

Last year the Stearns-Knight car was the choice of a thousand men—men who search the markets of the whole world, and demand the best.

All of them, practically, were experienced motorists. They knew the inherent faults and complications of the poppet valve motor. They knew, too, of the remarkable records made by Knight type motors in the leading foreign cars.

These thousand men took our entire output. Others of their class waited for us to offer a car of greater power. Now we announce such a car—

THE SIX-CYLINDER STEARNS-KNIGHT

In sheer, exhilarating power this new model is a worthy successor to the old 30-60 H. P. Stearns — one of the greatest cars the world has ever known. In silence, flexibility and ease of control, in comfort and convenience, it is a supreme achievement in motor-car luxury.

The equipment is absolutely complete. It includes Gray & Davis electric starting and lighting system, Warner Auto-meter, top, windshield, Mea magneto, Klaxon horn, demountable rims, and many other appointments.

Seven-passenger Touring Car	:	$5000
Five " " "		4850
Four " light " "		4850
Three " Roadster		4850
Limousine	.	6100
Landaulet		6200

Catalog and descriptive matter upon request

The F. B. Stearns Co., Cleveland, Ohio

Branches and Dealers
in 125 Principal Cities

Stearns
THE ULTIMATE CAR
(KNIGHT TYPE MOTOR)

LEADERS OF MEN   THE ARMY

ENVY

THE KIND OF convertible to buy depends on what you want out of a car and what you hope your dollar is buying. There's a variety of types, models and sizes, and what you're looking for is a matter of what you're looking for.

ECONOMY. No subcompacts and only a handful of compacts were made with cloth tops; and with the exception of the VW bug, only sheer luck will deliver you a solid ragtop that gets over 20 miles per gallon. There were no Pinto, Vega or recent small AMC converts at all. Dodge Darts and Plymouth Valiants held their own on mileage but weren't big-production items and have grown scarce. Ford Falcons and Corvair Monzas are more findable ragtop compacts, but their economy value may soon send them into the collector category. Among mid-size converts, mileage varies by individual car.

RELIABILITY. Beginning in 1973 with the semi-experimental attempts to meet federal safety-emission requirements, repair-incidence records of American cars went crazy. No two were identically trust-

worthy, and the last year for which you could make flat statements about mode/realiability was 1972. In the early '70s, the best repair records were compiled by the Buick Skylark and Century, the Chevy Monte Carlo, the Dodge Dart 6, the fullsize Ford and Mercury, the Merc Comet, the Olds Cutlass/F-85, and the Pontiac LeMans. Before 1970 you're talking about cars of eight years' vintage and more, for which reliability is a function of the automobile in question, its history and condition.

APPRECIATION. This involves time, study and a ton of factors: price, model, restoration potential and projected costs, traditional marketing qualities, showmanship quotient, rarity, elan, styling and options. If you're seriously thinking of investment-buying, read the "Head In The Clouds" section of this book and prepare to spend several months becoming market-wise. This is no low-rent game.

There are a few general rules, though. Because Ford products—from Model T's to Cobras—so whoppingly dominate the hot-used-car market, any

Oldsmobile 15th Year

THE OLDSMOBILE SIX has been well described as "*a new car with old traditions.*"

New, because it represents the very latest and the very best in advanced improvements and refinements of body design, chassis and equipment; old, in the Oldsmobile traditions for rugged strength and confidence inspiring ability—traditions of fifteen years' standing. . . . We believe this combination is practically unique among manufacturers of high grade six-cylinder cars—and worth the critical analysis of every purchaser.

Power and flexibility is a dominant feature,—slow travelling on direct drive, with smooth and especially rapid acceleration. Thus the car is a delight to handle, in traffic or on the open road.

While lighter in actuality as well as appearance, the car will "hold the road" and resist skidding on account of its balance and low center of gravity.

The long low body lines, wide doors and sloping hood are of entirely new design. The equipment, briefly specified below, is more luxurious than ever. The new and lower prices for the Oldsmobile are based on increased factory developments and economies, and the car, in appearance and performance, is one of the most successful "sixes" on the market.

The Delco self starter, lighting and ignition system, the best known positive device, is regularly used. The eighty ampere hour storage battery has sufficient energy to drive the car on electric source only. A power driven air pump for tire inflation is attached to the motor.

Seven Passenger $3350.   **Five Passenger $3200.**   **Four Passenger $3200.**

Complete equipment—Delco self starter, lighting and ignition system, cape top and boot, rain vision wind shield, Warner speedometer and clock, Truffault-Hartford shock absorbers, Klaxon combination warning signal, extra tire rim, demountable rims, power air pump, coat rack, complete outfit of tools, 135 inch wheel base, 36 x 4½ tires, 60 inch springs, luxurious upholstery 12 inches deep.

We have direct factory representation in all the principal cities, and dealers from coast to coast who will be pleased to show you this model—or write for catalog to the

OLDS MOTOR WORKS, Lansing, Michigan

given Ford ragtop will appreciate faster than a comparable alternative; but it will also be appropriately overpriced when *you* buy it. Chevrolets are in the same basic category, on a less painful level. Cars seldom seen on the highway are good bets to rise rapidly in value, as are those with near-mint bodies. The older the car, the closer it is to antique status, but when that finally happens, its price tag understandably explodes.

You'll be helped by a good sense of intuition—an ability to distinguish cars which have a unique flair or character, or which inspired deep affection and were unusually distinct or popular when new. But unless you have money to burn, avoid those which inspired fanaticism—like the Mustang and '57 Bel Air—for their sellers will not know reason. This intuition, like the ability to swim, can only be aroused and put to work by jumping into the water. 1953 Chryslers with "only" 85,000 miles and 1969 El Dorados with disintegrating seats, bent grilles and engines in the Last Rites stage are considered plums by sane, mature, respected used-car dealers. Obviously, plumhood is in the eye of the beholder, and the logic applied to evaluating the late-model transport car is void where classic units are concerned; and oddities like the ragtop enter this category several years sooner than ordinary hardtops.

A good argument can actually be made for luxury cars. Sure, they'll devour an extra $1.00 a year in gas, and repairs and parts will make coffee look like a bargain. But pricewise you can strike a much better deal for the shunned high-priced oldie than a used compact or pony car. Luxury models suffer from the current big-is-bad ethic, which makes them a slow turnover item. They usually teem with power options, much-prized by collectors and others with money to spend. As a rule, they'll have been better maintained and driven than the knockabout family items. They represent heavy investments by persons who tend to appreciate investments. And a higher proportion of status cars were made with cloth tops to begin with, meaning they and their parts are easier to find. On the other hand, power options and convenience features are invitations to trouble and repair work; and the bigger and more luxurious the convert—the more comfort and insulation—the less sense of excitement and animation derived from tooling it around.

In the final analysis, the only one who knows what kind of ragtop you want is you.

MOTORIST (*proposing*): Dearest, I adore you! Will you be my back-seat driver?

The Problem of the Used Car

By Robert Benchley

WITH the introduction of the new Ford car next month (or maybe it has been brought out already. I don't follow the papers very carefully), the problem of the used car becomes a national menace comparable only with the old plague of the seven-year locusts. It was bad enough before—as what wasn't?

For years, automobile manufacturers have been confronted with the problem of what to do with the second-hand cars turned in for new ones. The fact that they have given any money at all on second-hand cars shows what a public-spirited crowd the manufacturers are. It is like giving money for the return of water on the knee. When they get their old cars back, what are they to do with them? They can't eat them—that is, not unless they have been boiled down to practically nothing.

Some one has suggested that they be filled with potted plants and used to decorate the public parks, or stuffed with almond meats and used as favors. There is no sense in discussing these solutions. They are obviously too silly. However, we may come back to them if we can't think of something else.

CERTAIN it is that there are a great many more used cars than there are used drivers. A dealer in the Middle West had so many used cars out behind his garage that he closed his house and brought his family down to live in the cars—one car for the living-room, one for the dining-room and, without mentioning any names, one for brushing the children's teeth in. The only trouble was that the smaller children kept falling off the running-boards and hurting themselves and it was difficult getting the winter's coal into the car used for the cellar. The coal men had to toss it in, piece by piece.

Of course, the dealers sooner or later send the used cars back to the factory, but that just puts the problem off on the factory. A factory is supposed to make cars—not serve as a Bide-A-Wee Home for them. Several factories have had to suspend operations on new cars altogether in order to make room for the old ones. This was perhaps overdoing the sentimental phase of the thing a bit, but with the growing tendency toward sentimentality and service in business we are going to find more and more manufacturers who just haven't the heart to turn old cars out on the street when they come straggling home.

THE sentimental side of a second-hand car is one which has never been brought out sufficiently. It is not so much the wear and tear which a car has been subjected to during its years of service that makes it difficult to dispose of it. It is the ghosts and memories of former owners which infest its curtains and cushions and make it a veritable haunted house of old associations. I have had dealers tell me that on a still moonlight night they can hardly sleep because of the whistling and clanking which go on among the old cars behind the garage, spirits of Christmas Past and Summer Vacations of years gone by, which flit in and out of the sedans and roadsters, making night hideous for people in the vicinity.

One dealer, braver than the rest, went out one night and poked around among the used cars to see where the noise was coming from. He found nothing.

SEVERAL manufacturers have asked me: "What are we to do, Bob?" And my answer always has been: "What would Lincoln have done? (Not the Lincoln Company—the other Lincoln.) You manufacturers are confronted by one of the big problems of the age. Let's sit down and talk this thing over sanely, as one man to another."

And when we sit down, we always come back to the suggestion, discarded earlier in this study of the situation, that the used cars be stuffed with almond meats and used for favors. But then, a lot of people don't like almonds.

Theory *vs.* Practice

"LOVE," says the cynic, "is hollow."
  "Love," says the skeptic, "is rare."
  "They who heed Cupid,"
  The grouch says, "are stupid."
  The bachelor adds, "Love's a snare,
Nothing but catch-as-catch-can, sir—
  Woe to him caught in its whirls!"
Youth, tasting bliss, does not answer—
  His lips are pressed to his girl's!

Arthur L. Lippmann.

Between Pumps

MOTORIST: How do you figure that five gallons of gas at twenty cents a gallon make a dollar and six cents?

FILLING STATION ATTENDANT: The price went up to twenty-two cents before I put in the last three gallons.

WAS it mere coincidence that "Abie's Irish Rose" and the old Ford went out together?

ONE ADVANTAGE OF BEING FAT

THE WIDESPREAD PRESUMPTION that American cars are lemons and rattletraps just doesn't wash in the hard light of automotive day. Any honest mechanic, or, failing one, any consumer agency will tell you that you can get 100,000 miles out of almost any car made in the USA just by staying out of major collisions and maintaining it according to the owner's manual.

Indeed, maintenance is two-thirds of value and appreciation. Far and away the single greatest cause of auto deterioration and malfunction is the driver's reluctance to perform the simple functions of tune-up, oil change, transmission-fluid and cooling-system checks, tire rotation and wheel balancing/alignment. These cars were built to take good old-fashioned batterings and only failed to do so when markedly neglected. Says one collector: "Any car, if you overdrive it, will give you a problem. A car should be paced on its ability and the way it's built. The manufacturer tells you what the top speed is; don't try to go faster. The secret to these beautiful original cars is that they've been maintained properly in the manner they were designed to be."

A hundred thousand miles and long stretches of trouble-free performance are like good teeth and low blood pressure—they require nothing more than "preventive care." This won't heal all the maladies of age, of course, and there will be parts to replace. No sweat. These mid-'60s models came out of Motown in great floods, and for every one still on the road there are several in various stages of dismemberment in junkyards and auto salvage lots across the country, and theirs are some of the cheapest and most acessible replacement parts on the used-car market. Most major lines also continue to provide new parts for models no longer made.

Regular diagnostic checkups are the best substitute for a new-car warranty, insofar as they save repair money and increase owner-security and untroubled operation. Short of that, this list of Maintenance Musts is fairly standard and well worth committing to a schedule:

[1] Every week or so, check the level and condition of the oil, battery acid, radiator water, brake fluid, transmission fluid, windshield washer reservoir and the tire pressure and lights.

[2] Tune-ups produce better mileage and performance and should be done twice a year. Periodically

JUST as Cadillac beauty created a vogue in motor car style, so has Cadillac's incomparable performance re-created a vogue for driving. There is an irresistible desire to take the wheel of the Cadillac and enjoy what none but a Cadillac-built car, with its 90-degree, V-type, 8-cylinder engine, can give—performance seemingly unlimited in range and variety, so unlabored, so easily controlled, so zestful yet restful, that once again Cadillac has given the idea of luxury in motoring a new meaning.

More than 50 exclusive body styles by Fisher and Fisher-Fleetwood

CADILLAC
A NOTABLE PRODUCT OF GENERAL MOTORS

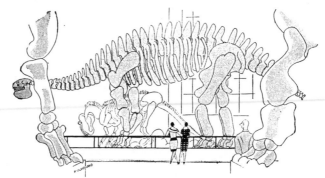

"Oh, Myrtle, what a wow of a radiator cap!"

between times pull the spark plugs and check them for oil, blistering or corrosion, and replace them accordingly. Replace spark plug cables every few years.

[3] Every 3000–6000 miles, depending on your owner's manual, the oil and oil filter should be changed and the chassis lubricated. Air and gas filters should be checked at this time and will want replacement once a year.

[4] Every autumn, have the radiator flushed out and the coolant/antifreeze replaced, along with the rust and corrosion inhibitor. While you're at it, get the water pump checked for noise and leaks, and replace any cracked or brittle hoses and fan belts.

[5] The fluid in the master brake cylinder should be no more than one-half inch below the top. The brakelines and linings should be inspected yearly. Brake adjustments are advised whenever the parking brake begins to slip or the brake pedal nears the floorboard.

[6] Battery fluid should be checked monthly, particularly in hot weather. Terminals and cable clamps should be kept clean and crud-free; wirebrush off any corrosion and coat the terminals with vaseline for protection. Watch for cracks. A weak battery fatigues wiring and the starter and is no place to skimp. Especially regarding older power-laden cars with automatic tops, a key to hassle-avoidance is a big, strong battery. Low-current jobs can mess up your entire electrical system.

[7] About every six months, go over the exhaust system and muffler for rust and holes. Shock absorbers have an average 20,000 mile lifespan and should be inspected accordingly; dip and sway problems when braking and turning want swift attention. The bigger the car, the greater the chances of problems in the suspension.

[8] Keep wheels aligned and tires balanced at all times.

[9] To avoid automatic transmission wear, change the fluid every 15,000 miles and use fluid specified in the manual.

[10] Some materials such as rubber parts and ragtop rear windows deteriorate constantly with time, not mileage. Look them over regularly. Small scrapes on metal and tears in cloth tops rapidly become big rust spots and gashes. A stitch or dab of paint in time saves plenty.

[11] If the car at any time in any way starts behaving differently or unusually, find out what gives at the nearest reliable mechanic.

[12] Respect the cloth top on your car as you do the roof on your home—it's your overhead protection. Tops are much easier to replace than one might think. Any upholsterer can custom-make one for $100–$300—luxury tops may run $500–$700—and persons specializing in this craft are almost everywhere. C.J. Whitney lists them for all 1947–75 American cars for as low as $40, and Sear's is reputed to have one for every convert since 1941. In any case, have a professional install the new top to insure a good fit, seal and appearance.

Automatic tops came into being with individually-motorized screw-jack affairs in 1940. These were replaced by hydraulic systems in 1946. On some of the '60s models, such as the Firebird, you could get a manual top as an option, but the odds are you'll have an automatic. With age you'll want to watch for weak seals and possible leaks in the hydraulic system, which should be kept filled with brake fluid. Other than the small T-Birds, few one-man tops really *were*, and a can of oil and rust-inhibitor will often come in handy on the raise-lower mechanism joints.

THE BRUNN CONVERTIBLE VICTORIA ON THE STORM KING HIGHWAY

THE LINCOLN

One Lincoln owner, during an active life, has purchased and driven forty-seven motor cars. That he recommends his latest purchase, the Lincoln, to friends who seek his judgment as an engineer, is a sincere and convincing tribute to the car's excellence. The Lincoln appeals most of all to the experienced and the critical. . . . The new Lincoln is a superb fusion of the engineer's and the coachmaker's arts. The famous 12-cylinder motor is of the V-type, and ranks first among Lincoln contributions to engineering. In comfort, the car surpasses even its forerunners — long, soft springs, a position close to the road for so large a car, luxurious upholstery and the silent surge of the engine make each journey tireless and refreshing. Front and rear fenders are in the spirit of the new streamlining, with the fresh, clean sweep of sloping contours. But here, too, is traditional Lincoln dignity. Appointments throughout are wisely and thoughtfully chosen. There are eighteen body types, formal and informal, including custom coach designs by Brunn, Judkins, Willoughby and Le Baron.

Any car will begin costing repair money by about 50,000 miles, but each make tends to have characteristic weaknesses and trouble-spots, and these should receive closer-than-average scrutiny. For example, alternators were a weakness of American Motors, Chrysler and Ford. Let's break this down by corporation.

American Motors—The engines and transmissions were basically strong, but electrical systems were prone to crankiness. You probably won't find an AMC ragtop available anyway.

Chrysler Corporation—Rugged engines and transmissions, but with a tendency to radiator leaks, starter problems and alternator-threatening wiring flaws. Ignition systems on Dodge V8's were cranky; ditto fuel lines. Post-1970 Dart and Valiant manual transmissions aren't recommended. Slant-six engines were marvelous workhorses but some developed valve-cover leaks. Pre-1970 Dodge brake cylinders were known to leak after 20,000 miles, and almost anything that could go wrong with a big Chrysler did. Trouble-spots: locks, handles and latches (1969–71 Plymouth); wind/noise leakage (1970–71 Plymouth, all Dodges); drivetrain (1969–71 Plymouth, post-1970 Dodge V8); electrical (1969–70 Plymouth, all Dodge V8s). Most trouble-prone: Chrysler V8's; 1969–71 Coronet V8; 1969–70 fullsize Dodge V8; 1969 Tempest; 1970–71 Barracuda V8; 1970 Satellite; 1970 fullsize Plymouth. Most trouble-free: 1965–71 Dart 6, especially 1969; 1965–69 Dart 8; 1965–67 Coronet; 1965–70 Valiant, 1965–68 Barracuda 6; 1965–67 Belvedere; 1965–66 fullsize Plymouth.

Ford—Wonderfully durable engines, particularly the 289. The automatic trans on small V8's and 6's, especially in pre-1970 Fords, would commonly fade at 40,000 miles, and all Fords were weak in the clutch. Pre-1970 Mercs were hard on shock absorbers, and Mustangs went through them at a hellish rate. Brakes and suspension are to be watched in general, as are radiator hoses on all V8's. Post-1968 Cougars were hotbeds of suspension and electrical problems, and smaller Ford/Merc U-joints may need repair as early as 35,000 miles. Trouble-spots: cooling system (pre-1970 Fords/Mercs); short-life engines (pre-1970 Fords). Most trouble-prone: 1967–71 Cougar V8; 1970–71 Mustang V8. Most trouble-free: 1968 Falcon 6; 1969–70 Falcon 8; 1965–67, '71 Comet; 1969 Montego; 1970–72 full-size Mercury V8.

GM—Expect radiator leaks and U-joint troubles on Buicks any time after 35,000 miles. Cooling-system leaks afflicted all Chevys, pre-1970 Buicks and big Oldses. GM suspension always bears watching; Tempest/GTO rear springs could go after 20,000 miles. Water pumps on Chevy 6's were only reliable for 20,000 miles, and some carburetors were hard to adjust for a smooth idle. The Chevy 327 had cam troubles, a $200 matter. Most GM cars tended to carburetor and starter hassles. Trouble-spots: alternator (Olds V8); corrosion (pre-1970 Chevys, all Pontiacs); wind/noise leakage (Chevys); short-life engines (pre-1970 Pontiacs); fuel line (pre-1970 Chevys and Oldses); drivetrain (pre-1970 Buicks); shocks (pre-1970 Pontiacs and Oldses); manual trans (Chevys); automatic trans (pre-1970 Chevys). Most trouble-prone: 1967–69 Chevelle; 1969, '72 Camaro; 1965 fullsize Chevy V8; 1966–70 Tempest; 1967–68 fullsize Pontiac V8. Most trouble-free: 1965–68 Buick Special 6; 1965–72 fullsize Buick V8, especially '69–70; 1969–72 Skylark; 1965–72 Olds F-85, especially '71; 1965–72 fullsize Olds V8, especially '70; 1967, '70 Toronado.

VW—Beneath the used Bug's battered-and-clanky image is an extremely sound and dependable automobile, but most mechanics will tell you that VWs tend to be the most beat-up and uncared-for cars in history. Thus a Bug's weaknesses will be more a matter of ownership than manufacture, and a well-maintained one is a rough diamond. Often, however, they'll have rebuilt or non-stock engines, most of which will need work and semi-constant tuning. Also, the VW wasn't designed for American driving punishment, such as big loads, high speeds and hot-rodding. But repair-wise, almost nothing can touch them.

Regarding hazards like vandalism, parking-lot damage, theft and collision, "preventive maintenance" means *insurance*. Most major companies make no special provision for convertibles and charge the same rates as for sedans—Allstate, Farmers, and State Farm, for example—but some (e.g. Farmers) expect special rates before long, and others (e.g. State Farm) may cover only 25–50 per cent of the top's replacement cost. All three of these outfits offer special policies for "keepers"—low-production or unique autos—and you're wise to get such a policy to cover the enhanced worth of your open car. Value is established up front through appraisal or a scan of the classifieds, and premiums are proportional to estimated real-market value. Rates vary by insurer, and some agencies can become quite picky, given the figures involved, and you'd better have a good driving record; two tickets in three years could cut you out.

Indeed, the basic rule underlying all forms of maintenance and investment-protection is to drive and treat your convertible as if it were worth everything you hope it is.

THE *Difference* IS MORE MARKED THAN EVER

Those who are not able to avail themselves of the rare privileges which Cadillac and La Salle owners enjoy, can still be better served than ever before by a number of excellent cars of lower price. ✓ ✓ ✓ The whole industry has moved forward — mostly in the direction of massed demand and sprightly appearance and performance; but, of course, Cadillac has been, as always, in the forefront of that forward movement. ✓ ✓ ✓ In fact, the difference and the distinction in Cadillac and La Salle have become more marked than ever, for Cadillac has deliberately planned its 1936 creations to widen the gap between the Royal Family of Motordom and all other cars in the world. ✓ ✓ ✓ Those who revel in the special ease and elegance and the pronounced distinction which Cadillac and La Salle provide for their owners, simply cannot satisfy themselves with anything else. ✓ ✓ ✓ The briefest of experiences, either at the wheel or as a chauffeured passenger, will prove this to your entire satisfaction.

*Model illustrated $1255. Monthly payments to suit your purse.
Prices list at Detroit, Michigan, subject to change without notice.
Special equipment extra.

La Salle
CONVERTIBLE COUPE *

[85]

YOUR NECK IS STUCK OUT.]

THE TYPICAL car-investor's fantasy involves picking up some rolling wreck for $500, bringing it up to line with $1000 worth of repairs or cosmetic surgery and winding up with a $3000 automobile. This is called doubling your money, and it makes Wall Street look like a dark alley —and it does happen! One Oakland collector recently bought with no argument a 1937 Packard Super-8 coupe roadster for $9500, spent about two grand on the top and interior and sold it for $23,000, all "within a matter of a month."

Investment-wise, age is everything. Pre-World War Two ragtops, most of which were driven to death during five years of no new cars, are gold mines. They were beautifully built, have compound dual carburetors on straight-8 engines which virtually flew and even restored have been known to hit 85 mph on mountain roads. A 1941 Buick Roadmaster convertible is a $12,000–$15,000 item if you can find one.

But you needn't go quite that far back to hit pay dirt. After about 15 years, the ugly duckling "used" car suddenly blossoms into the swan-like "vintage" auto. A 1947 Plymouth convert devoid of major external injury needn't do much more than *run* to be a good buy—mileage be damned; a clean one is worth $3000 anytime. The 1948 Continental, 1955 T-Bird and 1957 Bel Air are prime examples of postwar models now in the vintage phase. They're known in the trade as "strong" cars, which is an understatement. Unfortunately, they're also so rare, coveted and costly that only a dedicated collector with carloads of spare time and/or money can afford to even look for them, let alone buy them once located.

This game is tempting, but that doesn't necessarily make it right for you. Sauce for the goose can be strychnine for the gander, and the "collector's car" is riddled with drawbacks. Be prepared to worry about your gem at all times, to sprinkle extra security devices around it and to dash out panic-stricken to throw a tarp over it at the first hint of rain. Be ready to drive it very selectively, if at all, and to pay dearly

The Endless Chain

This is the Motor that Jack bought.

This is the House that was mortgaged to pay for the Motor that Jack bought.

This is the Mortgage upon the House that paid for the Motor that Jack bought.

This is the Lawyer who arranged the Mortgage upon the House that paid for the Motor that Jack bought.

This is the Motor of the Lawyer who arranged the Mortgage upon the House that paid for the Motor that Jack bought.

This is the House that paid for the Motor of the Lawyer who arranged the Mortgage upon the House that paid for the Motor that Jack bought.

This is the Mortgage upon the House that paid for the Motor of the Lawyer who arranged the Mortgage upon the House that paid for the Motor that Jack bought.

This is the Real Estate Man who arranged the Mortgage upon the House of the Lawyer who arranged the Mortgage upon the House that paid for the Motor that Jack bought.

This is the Motor of the Real Estate Man who arranged the Mortgage upon the House of the Lawyer who arranged the Mortgage upon the House that paid for the Motor that Jack bought.

This is the— But why continue? We all own Motors, and we all get them in the same way.

from LIFE, *January 9, 1913*

for replacement parts.

Get to know the signs of classic-car counterfeiting: fiberglas fenders, non-original engines and accessories sold as factory-stock, and so forth. Some bogus 1976 Bicentennial El Dorados have reportedly already been involved in five-figure rip-offs. And this phenomenon will get worse as the market gets better. Gird yourself for spending hours learning the ropes at auctions, swap meets, rallies, car club meetings and *concourses d'élégances*. Subscribe to *Hemmings*. Pitch a tent in the automotive section of the library. Then begin your long and patient hunt.

When you find what you want, in most cases it'll belong to someone who doesn't want to sell just yet or at current prices. But even persons who swear they'll never sell their prizes, will—for a variety of reasons and non-reasons, often without warning, and sometimes at bargain prices. Wait and wait and wait, and keep inching your offer upward until the owner breaks. Sheer persistence often nails down a pearl at half the market value.

Nine out of ten pearls, however, are already owned by collectors, whose prices will obliterate your appreciation. The few pre-'60s ragtops available from mortal owners are going to be pretty banged up, and making them into 90-point cars—top restoration numbers—can become as endless a task as tax reform and only slightly less complicated. One Cadillac fanatic recently passed up a rare 1958 Cad convert simply because it needed too much work. Under almost no circumstances should you tackle a full restoration job unless you plan to spend several years at it, or have done it before and feel experienced, or personally know a good mechanic, upholsterer, and body repairman. Even major restoration of 1960's cars, given labor costs and major parts, becomes prohibitive.

The solution is to settle for something fairly recent which doesn't *need* restoring; a complete, mechanically sound car with reasonable mileage and a good track record. For that matter, the criteria for a good transportation car and a good investment car overlap, and if you can find the former, it will ultimately become the latter. Common basics are low mileage, sturdiness and good physical condition. Transportation convertibles most likely to become collector's items are those with unusual styling, original factory material, less than 75,000 miles, and well-groomed interiors.

However, where transportation only requires mechanical reliability, collection-quality demands near-mint condition. The engine is less of a concern to the collector, since it can be rebuilt without affecting the car's value, but things like non-factory seats and fenders are a big deal. Collector-buying emphasizes body purity, especially on slab-slide or molded-side cars. Once they've been dented, the metal is stretched and almost impossible to return to original form; so the connoisseur will take a pristine body with a dead engine over the reverse any time. Also, mechanical repair is cheaper and easier to have done than major bodywork and new interiors. Good performance means good transportation; good appearance means good investment. A combination is dynamite.

Note, though, that on a vintage ragtop a mint exterior is worth $800–$1000, and an interior in showroom condition about the same; and these are the most fragile elements of any car, especially when used for routine transportation. It quickly becomes unwise for a non-collector to drive something so valuable and vulnerable on a regular basis, and the better your convert looks, the greater the prospects will be that it will spend most of its time in your garage. This puts you back on the street looking for a ragtop you can drive around and have fun in, which is where we started, and why.

Even if you settle for a purely transportational/recreational car, it doesn't hurt to keep one eye on such factors as future popularity and marketability. Not all ragtops are created equal, and they vary in appreciation-potential in ways you can perceive and predict. Big Oldses and Dodges are slow-market items right now with little seller advantage, while for Mustangs and Cutlasses you could get actual blood. Generalities are a fast way to make mistakes, but there are several *types* of convertibles which can still be expected to rise steadily in value.

[1] *Little* Convertibles. These items get hotter with each day of the energy crisis; as it intensifies, so will their value. In 1977, some Cougars and Firebirds were selling for more than their top-line luxury contemporaries. But few small ragtops were made; thus they're hard to find and even harder to find at uninflated prices. One collector sold a ten-year-old 1966 Corvair with 118,000 miles for $2650—just $100 under its original new-car cost. That's the kind of market you're working with here.

[2] *Ford* Convertibles. Since day #1, Ford products have dominated car collecting almost to the point of *carrying* it. There are a lot of reasons for this: the Model A and T are the overwhelming majority of all antiques; everyone seems to have a Ford somewhere in his family or past; it was most often a convertible fancier's *first* convertible. As a result, almost any clothtop Ford is money in the bank. One collector bought a '66 Mustang in 1976 for $1100 and sold it a year later for $2650 without laying a hand on it. An undistinguished 1962 Galaxie convertible bought in 1975 for $200 and given $200 worth of repairs sold in 1977 for $1200.

It's gotten to the point of much bitching and fuming among connoisseurs that Fords and Mercurys have become overpublicized and, accordingly, overpriced. But this just distills out to the basic complaint that more and more outsiders are discovering the used-Ford game. No one really knows *what* is overpriced. Ten years ago, people buying 1955–57 T-Birds for $1000 were told they shouldn't sign things without a guardian; in 1977 the same cars in mint shape were being appraised at up to $20,000; if it has the original power seat motor, name your price. A Cougar or Mustang could be overpriced at $3000–$4000 and still go on to hit $5000. Ford products are simply the blue-chip stock of this market for the cautious fun-car speculator, and while they may peak out for periods, they're almost sure bets at least to hold their own value in the long run.

[3] *Other* Convertibles. Since most ragtop-hunters are Ford-obsessed, this is a fine opportunity for you to take advantage of the relative buyer's market in non-Fords. A Shelby Mustang GT-350 commonly goes for around six grand; a Chevy Camaro Z/28 with almost identical credentials is lucky to draw half that amount. There are scores of such cases. Go pour through mid-'60s car magazines for road tests comparing hot-shot Fords with the competition; look for those of similar design and with competitive performance stats, and it's hard to miss a good deal. But first check the classifieds for non-Fords which are also growing too rich for your blood—there are already ads by persons looking for Buick Electras and Pontiac Firebirds.

THERE IS NO ironclad formula to determine the dollar appreciation of a car since no two are alike, but anything which can pass this quick test will probably graduate in value. There are 16 questions, and the right answer to each one is "Yes."

[1] Does the car need less than $250 in repairs or overdue maintenance?

[2] Is it a one-owner car?

[3] Does it have less than 75,000 miles on the odometer?

[4] Does it by any chance have less than 50,000?

[5] Dare we ask—less than 25,000?

[6] Was it widely popular—or notorious—when new?

[7] Did it cost a lot of money for its time?

[8] Was it unusually economical?

[9] Is it all, or almost-all, original material?

[10] Were less than 2500 of the model produced that year?

[11] Is it any Ford, or a GM car with a good sales record?

[12] Is it a high-performance or muscle car?

[13] Was it mechanically remarkable for its time?

[14] Was (or is) it considered stylish in design?

[15] Was the convertible body different from the body on the same model's sedan?

[16] Was it the first, or the last, of a line?

Grading For Investment:

Seven points—It should probably be bid on, especially if answer #1 was a Yes, but not beyond about 65 per cent of its new-car price.

Ten points—If it's a Ford, it may be *worth* the new-car price; if not, it's still worth the high current price.

Twelve points—Sutter's Mill; try not to leave without it.

(Add a bonus point for mint condition—zero wear, under 20,000 miles—which raises car value about 25 per cent across the board.)

Grading For Transportation:

Five points—If it's a 1965 model or later and runs well, it should give you several years of relatively untroubled driving pleasure and may even return a profit when you hand it along. At the least, given the eternal hard-core for whom life is incomplete without a convertible, you'll be able to get more for it than for the comparable sedan.

Seven or more points—You'll get your money's worth either driving it, reselling it, or both.

*Posed with 1935 Buick Series 90
Convertible Phaeton: Al Jolson and Ruby
Keeler, with Director Bobby Connolly and the dance
cast of Warner Brothers' new production, "Go Into
Your Dance." Buicks are used in "The Goose and
the Gander," "Caliente" and "A Night at the
Ritz," Warner Brothers' latest pictures.*

On the Silver Screen..where the Styles are set
. . . *Buick plays the lead !*

Style of a motor car in the pictures must be modern and individual. So Hollywood—originating the brilliant styles which a nation adopts from the screen—chooses Buick for big hit productions. Modish in the spirit of these sophisticated times, this beautiful Buick style is worthy of your inspection—just as it is worth the while of your motor car investment to take out a 1935 Buick for a trial drive. It is one thing to have style. But it is quite another to have, along with it, the quality and performance, the dependability and safety of a

Buick. Luxury of room you want, too, with the smoothness of Buick's Knee-Action gliding ride and the security of safety brakes and safety glass. In Buick you enjoy the unprecedented ease of many automatic features, sureness of control, and performance which you will list as the most polished in all motoring. Twenty-five beautiful models in four series, $795 to $2175, list prices at Flint, Michigan.

Prices subject to change without notice. Special equipment extra. Favorable G. M. A. C. terms.

Buick
1935

$795
and up, list prices at Flint.

WHEN   BETTER   AUTOMOBILES   ARE   BUILT,   BUICK   WILL   BUILD   THEM

MORAL

DON'T TRY TO KISS HER WHILE SHE IS DRIVING THE MACHINE

—A DISCLAIMER.⟧

THERE ARE MANY rules-of-thumb in this game: every dollar you put into renovating a convertible increases its market value by $2; ragtops will never actually decrease in value; etc. But rules were made to be broken, and it's still possible to take a third-degree burn in this market. There's often a thin line between making a killing and committing fiscal suicide.

A prime example is the 1976 open El Dorado, which was whipped into the $17–$25,000 range before it even left the showroom; within six months, undriven mint models were selling for upwards of $40,000. And the special Bicentennial version—nothing more than a white convertible with blue exterior accent stripes and a red interior trim package—was getting a numbing $100,000 from some sources. Ads in major classifieds all but pled for the opportunity to buy one.

By late 1976 this car looked better than a Swiss bank account, but there were those who warned that of the 14,800 in existence, 800 were on the road and 14,000 were in storage to drive prices up. Indeed, there were hundreds secreted in warehouses teeming with alarm systems and attack dogs around the land; speculators had bought them in multiple lots, and there were private mothball fleets of 30 and more. A Michigan Caddy dealer paid $19,500 each for nine of them; a New York dealer bought every Bicentennial model he could get for $40,000 each—almost one-fourth of the 200 made.

But by March 1977, this artificial scarcity—the coffee cartel of ragtoppery—caught up with these speculators, and 1976 ElDo prices sank like a Liberian tanker; some with under 6000 miles were being offered for $15,000—by dealers! The car's gold rush data had virtually reversed itself in six months, one of the most stunning examples in years of the horror of overbuying. Items stockpiled at 30 grand were now selling for half that. If garages were skyscrapers, people would have been jumping off them.

Nor is this necessarily an isolated instance. At this writing, 1965–69 cloth Mustangs are advertised in the papers at prices ranging from $1850 to $3500—their new-car price—despite the fact that almost 300,000 Mustang convertibles were produced over that period—such a huge latent supply that their current value may be far out of proportion to their actual numbers, and a wrenching devaluation could be not far off, in which case many persons would be badly stung.

Always remember the first rule of any investment game: don't buy hot; buy pre-hot. And the only way to gauge heat is by getting into the kitchen and testing the temperature for yourself. It would be pointless here to suggest approximate fair values for particular used cars. Even under ordinary circumstances, inflation would make such figures obsolete before this book hit the stands, and since prices for any given car will vary by geography, condition and popularity/ investment trends, you're caught in a purely day-to-day market structure.

A possible economic forecast of the used-car market lies, ironically, in the new-car market. For instance, a new-car sales boom in 1978 would pour a large number of trade-ins into the used-car supply, and some of these would be convertibles. It would also remove from the used-car buying population those persons who bought new cars instead. Ragtops would be less affected than used cars in general, but would still obey the law of greater supply and lesser demand. This cuts two ways, of course. If you're looking for economy and performance, it's good news, since prices will tend to hold steady or even slightly decline over the short run, and you'll have more one-owner cars to select from. But if you're going for investment, ragtop appreciation will be sluggish for awhile, and you'll have to ride out some extra lag time before prices begin spiraling up again.

In either case, there is the economic insurance policy of an *absolute* limit to the American ragtop supply; and although there will be peaks and valleys, the total available numbers will consistently decline with time, which heals all rash moves sooner or later. Just keep in mind that investment is a game anyone can play, but speculation is only for those with spare capital.

"COME ON, BILLY, THAT AIN'T THE KIND WE WANT ANYWAY"

THERE ARE NO DIFFERENCES OF
OPINION ABOUT

the Royal Family of Motordom

By "Best Bets," we mean sound used cars which happen to be nice investments, not the reverse. They are all transportation cars, meant to be driven frequently, but they also are to be scrupulously maintained. Luxury cars and pre-1960's models have been omitted since most are impractical as routine transportation, although both categories were excellent mechanically and are bound to appreciate. Cars are listed here for *overall* desirability, from fuel economy to design. Beyond that, their "value" depends on your particular criteria. *Consumer Reports'* top ten won't look anything like *Motor Trend's,* but these cars will most likely be acceptable to both.

While we're on that subject, there are dozens of Best Buy lists around, but the very fact that they *are* around means the cars included in them will rise to premium prices. The key here is the one that opens all financial doors—an awareness of where the trends are headed, not where they now lie.

Pony Cars (1965 on). Half compacts, half four-seat "sports" cars, these were the closest thing to a blend of American highway engineering and sporting lines ever mass-produced by Detroit. They sold faster than Vegematics.

The Ford Mustang. ✩✩✩✩ In overall terms—buyer popularity, design, innovation, industry impact and performance—this is widely considered the most successful American car ever made. With the exception of the early T-Bird, it's the hottest used car on the market. 1965–67 "classic line" models are near-hysteria collector's items; 1968 and later models can be had much more cheaply and are probably better all-around driving cars—with the 289 V–8, they're potential 100,000-mile units. They could be overpriced right now, or never, depending on the future. Since some persons feel it has peaked out, the market may be "soft" for awhile. A million were made, but most were beaten into plowshares by young drivers. Extremely well-built and untroublesome, they gave rise to the "pony car" style and designation.

The Mercury Cougar. ✩✩✩✩ A heavy sleeper; Mercury's version of the Mustang and, being a first cousin, far closer in design and engineering than in used-car price. But not all that many were made, and it's already taking off. "If you find a little XR-7 Cougar with air and leather," says one collector, "you've got something that'll double in value in the next couple years." Expect repair bills with post-1966 models, however.

The Pontiac Firebird. ✩✩✩✩ This is a terrifically flashy little two-door sleeper which featured unusually smooth lines and almost no trunk to speak of. But it was remarkably dependable for a showy car, and remarkably showy for any car.

The Chevrolet Camaro. ✩✩✩✩ Another oversize sports car, this was one of the most popular automobiles of its time. Almost identical to the Firebird in dimensions, it was still big enough to use as a family car without costing full-size money. It was one of the great mixes of zip and utility. The 1968–71 Camaro Z/28 is especially well spoken of.

The Plymouth Barracuda. ✩✩ This was Chrysler Corporation's version of the Mustang. Its slant-six and 340 V–8 engines were marvelous, but it suffered the touchiness of a dragstrip car, which it was. But Barracudas tend to be incredibly low-priced for their miniscule numbers.

COMPACT CARS (1961 on). These cars got at least 15 miles per gallon, and in such fortuitous cases as the Falcon, more than 20. They all share the qualities of excellent driveability and better-than-average repair records.

The Ford Falcon. ✩✩✩ These should still get around 20 mpg in well-kept condition, and as of this writing are for sale at preposterously low sums. Amid the heavy hype for 1978 "intermediates," recall that this was the original small intermediate. Try to get the 289 engine, not the six. And skip those models once given to teenagers as throwaway items to be driven into the blacktop.

The Mercury Comet. ✩✩✩ For all practical purposes—and those are the ones you're concerned with—this is simply Mercury's version of the Falcon. But generally it was a housewife's car, not a high school car, and will generally be in better shape.

The Chevy Nova. ✩✩ A car of simple, sound construction and great durability, with a meaty engine which, with care, was good for 125,000 miles and was easily maintained. The small V–8 is preferable to the six, and pre-emissions models are superior; considered a good buy even at 80,000 miles. But owners tend to hang onto Novas, and they're not cheap.

The Olds Cutlass. ✩✩✩✩ A remarkable sleeper which was built like a destroyer but whose popularity has dropped almost from sight due to its mileage, which was figured in yards beginning in 1973. Nevertheless, it was a beautiful car with an equally attractive reliability-record and laudatory praise of mechanics in general. Clean, fast, sporty, fine-handling, it had no real drawbacks. One of the classic singles' cars.

The Buick Skylark. ✩✩✩✩ Most of what applied to the Cutlass also holds for the Skylark, which was really only markedly different in its logo. It is much more appreciated by professionals than by the masses and thus is often underpriced. The 1965–67 models were extremely well-built, with rocklike transmissions. Many are still pristine at 40,000 miles.

The Dodge Dart. ✩✩✩✩ One of the supersleepers. Its slant-six engine made the Ark look flimsy; it would almost literally run forever, and Dodge pickups with the same engine have gone 160,000 miles with no teardown. It was a rare combination of remarkable durability, economy and gas mileage. Hotly-praised by mechanics, who recommend the automatic trans, they're considered good buys as old as 1966 and up to 80,000 miles. Authorities call them 150,000-mile cars, and they may be the best values in this book for your dollar. The Torqueflite trans was spectacularly repair-free.

The Plymouth Valiant. ✦✦✦✦ Virtually identical to the Dart, with virtually identical references. It also shared a design relatively unpopular with buyers and collectors, but this only helps undervalue it. In early 1977, Valiants were available for $400. Outstanding transportation cars, Vals were safe, sturdy, and easily maintained. Like the Dart, they were family cars that just happened to have a cloth top, making them uniquely advisable to those who want a functional convert. But they can be almost impossible to find, and when they get hot—which they will—their market value will be ferocious.

The Chevrolet Corvair. ✦✦✦ "Take the Corvair . . . please." This was the prevailing attitude when this oppressed automotive minority was being sold in the '60s. Now, however, the word on the collector's pipeline is "Watch the Corvair." Some Monza Spyders are listing at new-car prices and are praised as "a great little car" by connoisseurs. Ralph Nader leveled such torrential consumer invective against it that its public image was simply *executed*. But much of this was PR overkill. The Corvair was actually GM's sincere attempt to adopt the better features of the VW, such as a rear-end, air-cooled engine; and it was more maligned than driven to death. It had a host of bugs, but most of the real clinkers have by now been weeded-out. The survivors are adventuresome, underrated little cars. But they were arcanely engineered and can be genuinely difficult and expensive to repair.

MID-SIZE CARS (1964–72). These weren't all that much larger than compacts and only seem big by current Honda Civic standards. They were built as dependable family cars, but with lines so racy they were later incorporated into muscle models. These were uniformly solid and attractive.

The Pontiac Tempest and *GTO.* ✦✦✦ The GTO had lines so sleek that even calloused auto writers used words like "esthetic." The handling was renowned, and the interior was unusually superb, with dead-solid fabrication and outstanding durability. Accessory-laden models are significantly more valued than stripped versions. 1964-65 GTOs may have been the cream.

The Olds Cutlass 442; the Buick Skylark GS; the Chevelle SS Malibu. ✦✦✦ These were other GM variations on the basic Tempest theme, and the same points apply, with minor deviations. One of the last functional combinations of size, economy and luxury, the Chevelle is particularly underpriced, and has a good repair record for all its conveniences. The Chevelle is a solid buy even at 75,000 miles. It and the Skylark are most likely to boom, say collectors.

The Dodge Coronet and *Plymouth Satellite.* ✦✦ Chrysler Corporation cars are notoriously ignored by collectors. No one knows exactly why this is, but it makes them marvelous buys, almost without exception. They have a reputation for functional durability but "tinny" bodies, meaning strong on the road but weak in the parking lot. They are perennial sleepers and an excellent place to start looking for stupendous bargains. Not that popular when new, they were still solid performance cars, and clean used models are as strong as steel and trapped in a buyer's market. Post-1968 sixes will probably want work.

The Ford Torino and *Mercury Montego.* ✦✦✦ The 1968–71 models were primo. Easier to maintain than their GM and Chrysler counterparts, their only notable weakness was suspension. Some of them got 15–20 mpg, and Torino sixes were especially reliable. The Montego is being called a "car to watch." Some feel they don't have the styling of the Chevelle and Skylark, but they make up for this with the bonus of Ford collectability.

BIG CARS (1962–70). Given the impracticality of luxury ragtops, this category is the top of the line for collectability and usefulness. Devaluated by the fuel scare, they are often better bargains than late-model compacts and mid-sizes.

The Chevrolet Impala. ✦✦✦✦. The 327 Impala V-8 was one of the great all-time bulletproof American cars, and one of the few non-Fords to be considered a classic while still being produced. It was probably the best-looking and most avidly-sought macho car of its decade, and mechanics still rate it at the top of its class in reliability; a strong buy even at 80,000 miles. Beautifully put together, and remarkably maintenance-free, it was the choice for an entire adolescent and young-adult generation. The crossed-flags emblem meant the big engine lay within.

The Buick Electra. ✦✦ Another sound sleeper, with the 1969 probably being the most desired by collectors. Mechanically strong and featuring unusually clean design, it will soon probably heat up among Buick devotees, a large club indeed.

The Dodge Polara. ✦✦ These are already beginning

..."it's the '49 FORD by a landslide!"

FORD has "MAGIC ACTION" KING-SIZE BRAKES

FORD has "HYDRA-COIL" FRONT SPRINGS

FORD offers "MAGIC AIR" temperature control

FORD has the "MID SHIP" ride

FORD has "PICTURE WINDOW" VISIBILITY

FORD has SOFA-WIDE SEATS

FORD gives up to 10% greater gas economy

FORD offers two great engines 100 hp. V-8 95 hp. Six

FORD has "DEEP DECK" LUGGAGE LOCKER 19 cu ft.

There's a New Ford in your future

JOY RIDERS

to move. Like most Chrysler products, they were especially sturdy, but Chrysler design in the '60s was spotty and frequently lacked zip, so it will continue to be undervalued by collectors for several years, which is a good enough argument for getting one. 1967–69 were the peak years.

The Mercury Monterey, ✡✡✡ The last big Merc ragtop, it is now quite rare. Very strong mechanically, visually and collectably, it's already appreciating rapidly on the west coast. It featured the size, comfort, handling and performance of a Lincoln—silent power—and still got up to 18 miles per gallon. Solid, practical transportation and probably the best dollar value in the big-car category. 1969's are the hottest.

The Ford Galaxie. ✡✡✡ A strong buy up to 60,000 miles and one of the quietest, best-riding cars ever made for its size; perhaps the best ragtop for car-stereo listening. Pre-emission-control performance and mileage make it an outstanding transportation car. With the bucket seats and floorshift, it was considered one of Ford's sexiest big cars, and was a visual knockout with the top down. The 1963/64 XLs are thought particularly well-engineered, with predictions of appreciation hitting $500 a year. Almost literally trouble-free.

THE BUG. The 1968–77 VW Beetle is in a class by itself. Older bugs are unusually good investments for transportation value alone—repairs are simple, inexpensive and easily done by the owner with manuals. It's probably the best buy on this list for sheer utility. What it lacks in chic and luxury it more than makes up for in old-shoe durability. As a knockabout

pleasure toy, it has no real peer. Its cloth roof was exceptionally solid, thick and quiet; it sealed better and was simpler to operate than 90 per cent of the competition. A good buy up to 50,000 miles; but avoid power options, air conditioning and the automatic trans. The 1967–70 models are highly regarded. Prices should bottom-out early in 1979, but, being somehow cute beyond devaluation, it could be a speculation car right now—witness the El Dorado phenomenon. A 1959 model with left-hand drive is the mother lode.

A CAUTION—Appreciation rates of many ragtops were already accelerating while this book was being written, and you're probably not the only one reading it and getting wild ideas involving early retirement. Some prices are going to soar insanely, ceiling-out and maybe even fall back precipitously. Which ones will do so is unpredictable, but any of these cars are strong candidates, simply because they're listed here. Early Mustangs already qualify as collector's items, and the GTO, Camaro, Firebird and Corvair are shoo-ins; they may all be too dear by the time you read this. Also, several cars, such as the Plymouth Fury, just missed making the list and should be considered as prospective sleepers. Remember—even a *best* bet is just that: a gamble.

Having admitted this, it's still true that any car you can get functional use out of, have a rare brand of fun in, feel extraordinary in while driving and maybe make a piece of change from in the end is simply a hell of a buy. Any knocking sound you hear is probably opportunity.

"TOWN AND COUNTRY"... Chrysler's work-or-play convertible ... magnificent in its utterly
new styling ... magnificent in the smooth, responsive power of Chrysler gyrol Fluid Drive
and improved hydraulically operated transmission ... another triumph of Chrysler's
imaginative engineering—first in the field with the developments that really matter!

the Beautiful Chrysler

FROM COAST TO COAST, SEE A
CHRYSLER-PLYMOUTH DEALER
FOR THE FINEST SERVICE

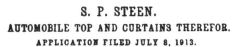

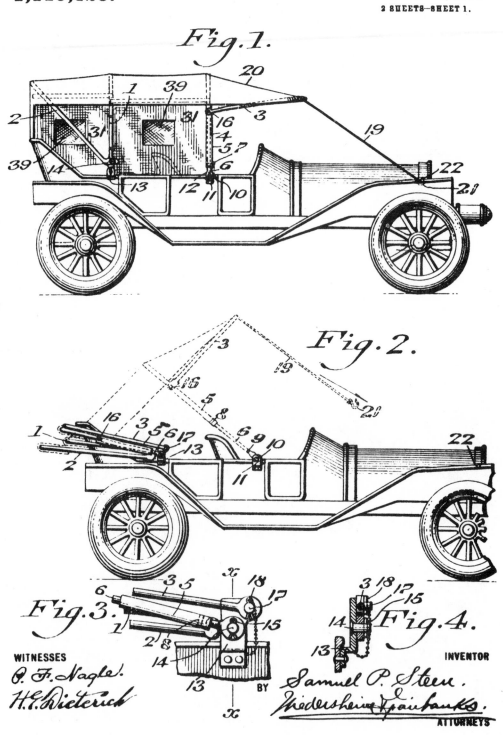

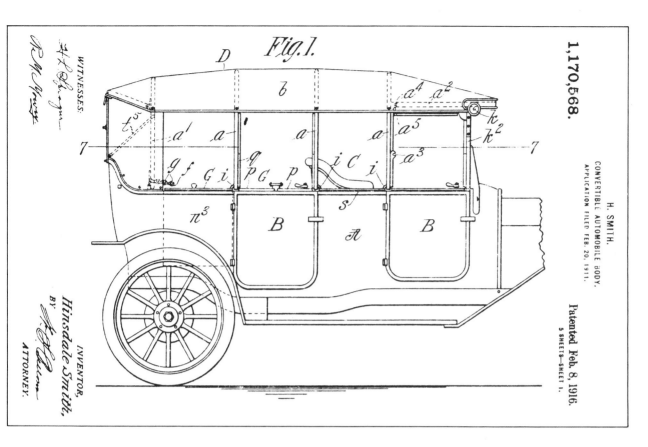

H. SMITH.
CONVERTIBLE AUTOMOBILE BODY.
APPLICATION FILED FEB. 20, 1911.

1,170,568.

Patented Feb. 8, 1916.
5 SHEETS—SHEET 1.

Fig.1.

WITNESSES:

INVENTOR,
Hinsdale Smith,
BY
ATTORNEY.

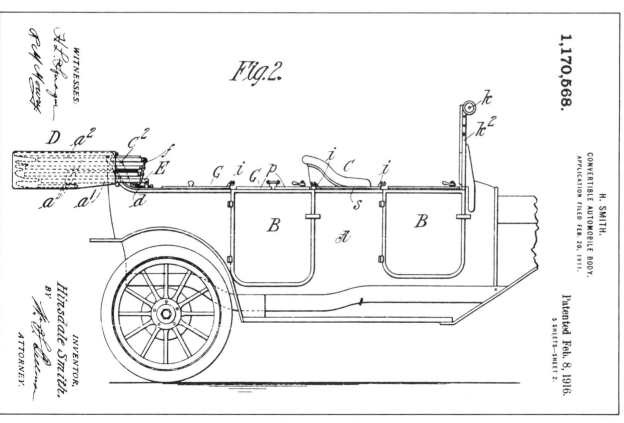

H. SMITH.
CONVERTIBLE AUTOMOBILE BODY.
APPLICATION FILED FEB. 20, 1911.

1,170,568.

Patented Feb. 8, 1916.
5 SHEETS—SHEET 2.

Fig.2.

WITNESSES:

INVENTOR,
Hinsdale Smith,
BY
ATTORNEY.

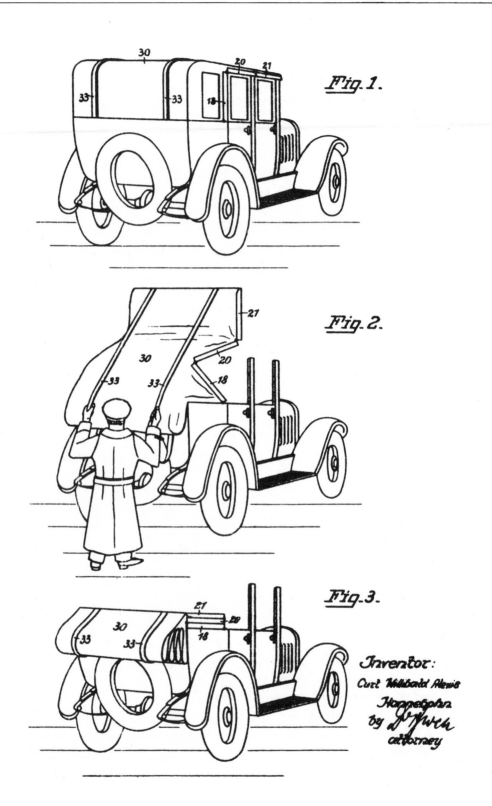

Fig. 1.

Fig. 2.

Fig. 3.

Inventor:
Curt Willibald Alewis
Hoppeßohn
by ‿ ᴊᴡᴄᴀ
attorney

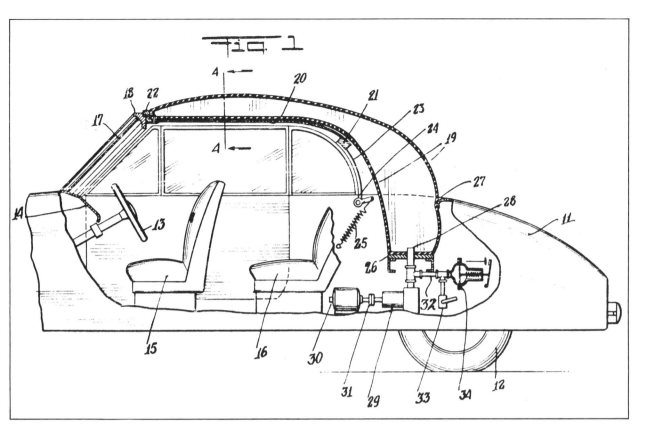

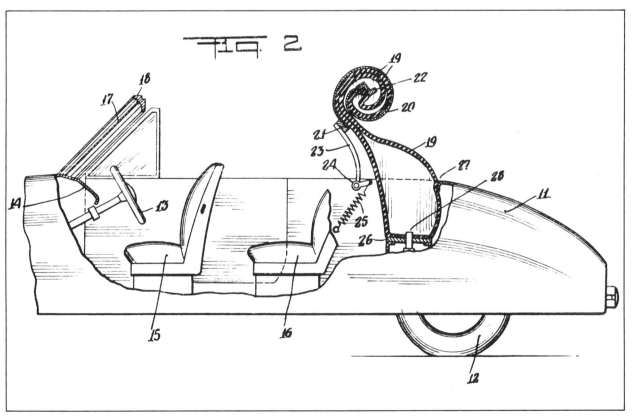

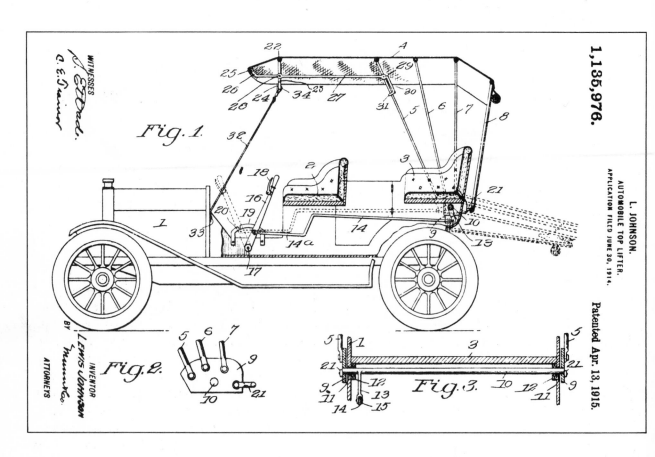

L. JOHNSON.
AUTOMOBILE TOP LIFTER.
APPLICATION FILED JUNE 30, 1914.

1,135,976.

Patented Apr. 13, 1915.

Fig. 1.

Fig. 2.

Fig. 3.

WITNESSES

INVENTOR
LEWIS JOHNSON
BY
ATTORNEYS

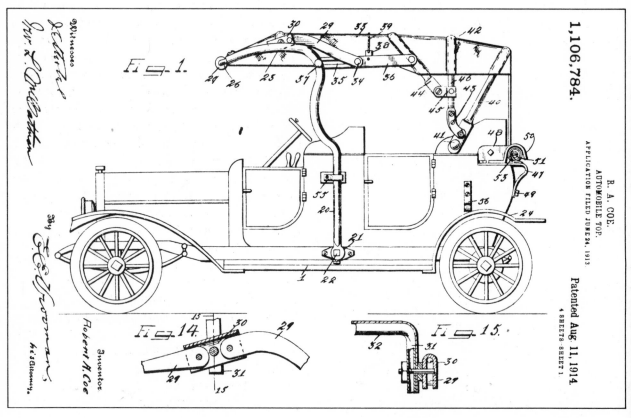

R. A. COE.
AUTOMOBILE TOP.
APPLICATION FILED JUNE 24, 1913.

1,106,784.

Patented Aug. 11, 1914.
4 SHEETS—SHEET 1

Fig. 1.

Fig. 14.

Fig. 15.

Witnesses

Inventor
Robert A. Coe

By

P ART OF THE GOODMAN collection in San Francisco, this unit was ordered in 1931 by a Peruvian millionaire who had the chassis shipped to Paris, where French coachbuilder Franay created the custom dual-windshield, four-door convertible body. Only one other exists, somewhere behind the Iron Curtain, originally built for the Queen of Yugoslavia. The J Duesenberg really played in a one-team league; nothing has actually approached it for preeminence and distinction. One of the finest performance cars ever built, it was a foot longer than any current Cad or Lincoln, and the 265 horsepower straight-8 could turn 120 mph without heavy breathing. The Franay body is distinguished by a huge rear-seat area with saloon-style foot-rests, leather rear-door saddlebags, pontoon-shaped rubber-inlayed wood running-boards, and hand-tooled everything. The teardrop fenders barely cover the tires, which are as big as wading pools. Just under 500 Duesies were made before the factory closed in 1937, but there may be as many as 300 on the road, museum-pieces all. This one came from an Arizona collector, is mint and unrestored, and is clearly a priceless example of what may have been the finest American motorcar in history. If there were any bidding, it would probably start at around $250,000, but this one is literally one-of-a-kind, with no peer—let alone superior, and there's really no ceiling to its dollar value. It was huge; the window frames rose five feet high and the headlights were a foot in diameter—but quick and responsive. The ultimate 1930's movie star car, it cost $20,000 new. Some were said to do 100 mph in seconds. In this car, you were no mere driver; you were Pappy Boyington.

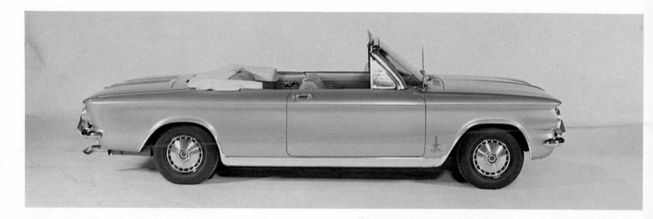

THIS WAS THE AUTOMOBILE Ralph Nader made this reputation on, and under his withering shafts of death-shot PR it became the Edsel of GM. He characterized it as a lethal rattletrap, but collectors scorn this as mostly overkill, and some vigorously defend the car. "Bulletproof," says one. "Basically a well-constructed car, and a lot of fun to drive . . . really a compact sportscar, very well built . . . and I feel to this day a safe car," says another. But other pros are less certain of its safety, and its engine could be a visitation like the plague. There's never been anything on the road just like that engine: it was in the rear, air-cooled, and thus free of cooling-system problems, but mechanically *unusual*, which can be as good as leprosy for a car's popularity and sales. The Corvair was designed as an economy car, but its unorthodox motor needed perpetual tuning unless you fed it the highest available octane. Some say that if GM had put the same development money into it that they spent on other projects, it could have been a goldmine. But some simple repair jobs required pulling the whole engine, which was vulnerable to rear-end shots in traffic, and the car, being unorthodox,

drew the loud ire of mechanics, who dislike exotic challenges and unusual methodologies and hated even seeing Corvairs drive in. Be all that as it may, the car is a collector's item. Few were produced, and given their adverse publicity, a vast number were quickly discarded. It's a flat statement that you can't find a Corvair clothtop on a car lot, and parts are out of the question. Bill Mainzer and Ruth Gelbart got this one the hard way—already restored from the original owner in 1976 for $1600. A ton of money for a car with 97,000 miles, but they've since turned down offers of $3500. They use it not for transportation but joyriding, which it delivers at 19 mpg. The rebuilt turbocharged engine is scalpel clean and runs flawlessly. It better. Ruth and Bill are particularly fond of the people who invariably ooh, ahh, and cluster around it. Indeed, whatever else you say about it, the Spyder combines the size and lines of a sportscar with the economy of a compact; and nothing else looks quite like it, which means a lot in this mania. Just remember the Corvair-owner's First Commandment: Carry fanbelts.

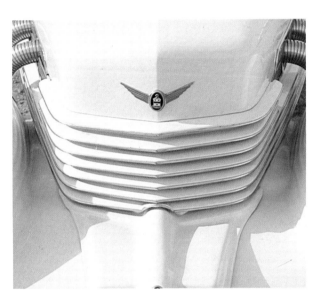

A LOT OF PERSONS deemed experts on the subject will tell you that designer Gordon Buehrig was the finest automotive craftsman America ever produced, and some visage of his coffin-nose Cord hangs on walls wherever the automobile is revered. One of the great American auto designs, it boasted a rare eccentricity—an electric gearshift; you just flipped it into the desired gear and pumped the clutch pedal once. There were also hand cranks on the dash to open and close the elegant retractable headlights, which worked like mini-awnings. Extremely fast, the Cord was equally as repair-prone. Another Golden Era movie star's car, it was remarkably clean-looking, and except for the massive segmented chrome exhaust pipes snaking out of the manifold, was virtually chrome-free. This one, owned by Charles Goodman, has 51,000 miles and an immaculate Errol Flynn-red interior. It was flung about by a Lycoming V-8 engine, and this is rumored to be the car cowboy star Tom Mix was killed in doing 120 mph in Arizona. It is unrestored, valued at about $35,000, and is still used for occasional joyriding. A plaque on the glove box reads: "This certifies that this Cord automobile has been driven 110.8 miles per hour before shipment," and is inscribed with the signature of Al Jenkens, presumably the test-driver. One of the superclassics, and of the most visually and mechanically remarkable quality cars ever made in America.

ABOUT AS LONG as a cabin cruiser, the last American convertible's "Bicentennial" series was distinguished only by a thin blue paint strip around the hood and back along the door, red interior trim strips and dashboard, and a small plaque inside which reads: "This 1976 Fleetwood El Dorado is one of the last 200 identical production convertibles." This would be a snap to counterfeit, and the word is that some unscrupulous types already have, as a sort of instant-collector's item is widely felt to be more hype, or at least manufactured novelty, than art. This one still carries the sales sticker on the window—$13,246—and a special letter authenticating it as a "Replica Convertible." In fact, it cost the owner $28,000 from the dealer—a nifty 15 grand markup. It's been warehoused since birth, but the paint is already beginning to fade and yellow in places. It has just 35 miles on it—accumulated when the car had to be returned to the dealer after the dormant battery ate through its casing. "A real rip-off," mutters the owner, who cares not to be identified. White elephant or not, it's never been rained on, and is 100-point mint, or lemon, depending. When you open the door, lights go on all over the interior. Dealers assured potential buyers in 1976 that it would be worth $15,000 as a trade-in in 1977. They were right.

OWNER AND FORD-COLLECTOR Lloyd Riggs describes this little rolling eclair as "an early-day hotrod." Young sportabouts who couldn't afford the then popular cars—the Mercer Raceabout and Stutz Bearcat—would take the old man's cast-off Model T frame and build up a racing engine for it such as this one has, with overhead valve conversion, Winfield racing carburetor and a few other odds and ends, and design and build their own body and fenders for it, finally coming up with what we called an "early-day speedster." This is one such, completely rebuilt from transplants: T frame, Eisenmann magneto ignition, a 3-to-1 rear end with a two-speed, and a body patterned after the 1913 Mercer. More a concoction than a restoration, there's nothing exactly like it on the road. It's a non-transportation showpiece and occasional fun car, officially a "Horseless Carriage." It gets 20 mph nonetheless and will do 70 mpg on the freeway, but Riggs is understandably edgy about going beyond that in a car weighing just 1200 pounds and worth "about $10,000." He did the restoration himself as a hobby, putting about $5000 in parts and labor into it over three years. The "windshield" is nothing more than a glass disc jutting up in front of the driver's face atop a vertical holding rod bolted to the steering-column. Seventy mph, you say.

THIS "CONVERTIBLE SEDAN"—meaning it had a sedan chassis and body and a cloth top—was a luxury car *in extremis*; owned by the Very Few. The rare four-door convertible car died out with this line in 1967, and 1964 is considered one of the best of its seven years. All big cars were basically open-road cars, and this is no exception, but generally it's felt to be even more driveable than its Cadillac contemporaries. This one, owned by David Bissel, is in "factory mint" condition with 116,000 miles on it, and almost nothing but a Continental could make that claim. Continentals absolutely teemed with power and convenience options, and there are still quite a few of them around, ranging in price from $2000 to $10,000. The top alone may be worth the price—it's something to behold: at the push of a button, the trunk—which was hinged in the *rear* over the fender—opened up, and this enormous batwing-like top accordioned out of it and arched up over the car. A sensor-device on the top's front end told the mechanism when it hit the windshield and an attachment clamp automatically came out and locked into place. The entire raise/lower operation involved 14 various switches, and the thing did just about everything but tell you when to turn it on. On the other hand, the trunk was totally filled by the top and therefore practically worthless, and the trunk-lid was known to jam in the upright position, where a good 30 mph airspeed was often enough to tear it off the car. Still, the mechanical process is an utter showstopper, and nothing else like it ever called so much attention to a single car and driver. Like most Continentals, it drove and handled like butter goes down your throat.

IN 1951, FORD heard that GM was coming out with a sportscar and went on a two-year blitz to design and build an American two-seat personal sportscar. The result was the Thunderbird, which was abandoned almost as soon as it was built, in favor of a more marketable four-seat model. The two-seat T-Bird's life was figured in months—only 53,166 were built from 1954–57, just enough to popularize the sportscar concept. To a remarkable extent, especially for Ford, it was a custom hand-made car; the body was built by the Budd Company, which made freight cars. For these and other reasons, it is one of the hottest collector's items in existence, authentic two-seat jobs selling well above their new-car price. Kathy Sparks is the third owner of this one, which has a rebuilt engine and trans, 139,000 miles, and three paint jobs. It cost her $700 in 1972, plus repairs, but is now probably worth $4500 minimum. She drives it for transportation "off and on," and gets offers for it wherever English is spoken. She's a housewife, not a collector. Is she the envy of her block? "Yes I am, ha ha ha. I'm very proud of it." The original Bird wire-wheels are almost nonexistent collector's items —one pro keeps his set under his bed. Kathy has the 1962 Bird wire-wheels, also hard to find, and cleans them in her dishwasher, "before you get down to polishing, and without the tires, of course." It was and is a matchless stares-and-reactions car but teemed with drawbacks, like blind spots in the rear side area, a two-man top, front-end weight which made it disaster to drive on wet/hilly streets, a packed-in engine which was tricky to work on, almost no head-room, and with such a tendency to admit rain that it was compared to driving a bucket of water. Its non-power steering handled like a truck, but it was still smooth-riding, heavy and safe, and unbeatable for open-road sunshine driving. And it is semi-priceless, which mitigates all sorts of faults. This one still gets 18 mpg.

THE MOST AMERICAN-IN-SPIRIT foreign car ever made, it's included here as a sort of naturalized automotive citizen. Probably the most ubiquitous ragtop on the highway, it was also one of the better ones. The cloth Bug introduced the glass rear window and defogger/defroster long before most other cars. The top is considered of Mercedes quality by some—thick, plush and solid, with excellent seal and insulation and above-average acoustics. Its snug fit is one of the best, and the cloth VW, being more squared off, has more headroom in the rear than the hardtop. It also has rolldown rear windows, which the Bug sedan lacks, and many feel it is the better of the two cars for design and comfort. And it was coachbuilt—all VW convertible bodywork was done by Karmann, of Ghia fame; thus open Bugs boast a higher level of finish and craftsmanship than their metal-topped brethren. Gaze upon it well, though, for this is the last of the breed, phased out for 1978. Its 1977 sticker price of $4849 included a four-cylinder fuel-injected engine, rack-and-pinion steering, four-wheel suspension, front stabilizers and a four-speed trans. Rated at 37 mpg on the highway, it's one of the few cloth cars which can laugh at, or at least grin and bear, the energy crunch. This, along with its emotional and perpetual popularity, makes the VW convert a virtual preordained future classic. This one came right off a showroom floor, with a license-plate holder reading, "I'm Cute and Dependable."

IN MATTERS OF SELF-DISPLAY, there is always the fine line between charisma and buffoonery. Driving astride that line is Nudie, of North Hollywood—Designer/Tailor to the Stars (Country & Western galaxy). Each year since 1950 he has let his conspicuous imagination work over a new American convert. Each year the result has been something like the 1975 GrandVille—the last open Pontiac—shown here. Nudie's notion of display inevitably involves western statuary, hand-tooled leather, a virtual carpet of silver dollars, and more mounted guns than a Coast Guard cutter—some of them included expressly to protect all the other regalia. Nudie's cars have more chrome than Uruguay, and probably are better suited to the Rose Parade than traffic. Ultimate open-car showpiece? Garish, tasteless excess? Beauty lies in the eye of the driver.

THE QUESTION NOW remains: Will the American convertible ever be built again? The answer seems simple, but the easiest answers are often the wrong ones. To assess whether or not the ragtop might return, we have to consider the factors which eliminated it from the automotive scene. One was *the scene itself*. Once, we went out and got into automobiles not as a reflexive act of going to work or the movies or the bank or the unemployment office, but simply to "go for a ride"; to drive with the hair in our faces and smiles like cathedrals upon our faces.

This was in 1950, however, when there were 20,000,000 registered passenger cars in the United States. In 1960 that figure was almost 62,000,000. By 1973 the figure was over 101,000,000, and "rides" were something to be found only in theme parks at $3.50 a shot. The degree to which driving was consistent with enjoyment decreased almost in direct proportion to the increase in automotive congestion. You couldn't get away from it all when it was all heading in the same direction you were. Nor could you run millions of people through an environment without trampling it, and the roadsides accordingly teemed with refuse, billboards and franchise clusters. City and suburban traffic was universally unbearable.

The other big change was in our *notion of self-display*. The theater of the highway has always been divided into spectators and performers, but the staging has changed dramatically since the last ragtop boom in 1965. It was just then, in fact, that the heavy-firepower mid-size luxury car, pony car and muscle car were placed by mass-production and a bull economy into the hands of the average driver. Suddenly cars named for animals and boasting more power than a sane man could ever use were The Thing. Openly sensual designs were advertised with open sensuality. Flashy embellishments—from racing stripes to opera windows—and lush option-laden interiors made any hardtop an affordable and unmistakable self-advertisement. Leather dashboards and quadraphonic sound replaced folding tops as indices of wherewithal, zing and attractiveness. Other new automotive life-forms offered functional alternatives to the open car. For these unrequited exhibitionists and free-spirits, there was that new horse, the motorcycle. For the flamboyant, there was offered a torrent of decor accessories to make even the most mundane car turn heads. For the narcissistic, there was that rolling canvas, the van.

Formerly, we drove cars which were literally open to the world—ourselves on parade, for all to see. Now we drive around in vans painted to look like Bryce Canyon, or in Olds Toronados with landau roofs, or in Dodge pickups with nine-foot CB antennae and gun racks, or in VWs plastered with provocative bumper stickers, or in cars with their names stenciled on the side and with 2000-decibel engines, or in superfly El Dorados. We've spared no expense or iota of ingenuity to recreate symbolically with walled-in vehicles what we once displayed openly and directly—which is, basically, ourselves. We're becoming a culture which worries over whether others will dislike our looks or perhaps stick a fist into them. We tend to wear masks. For transportation, we have mobile masks: the limousine for authority, the Porsche for prestige, the Toyota for common sense, the Barracuda for machismo, the 280 Z for allure and the van for billboard announcement of our presence. The three reasons one drove a ragtop were for enjoyment, for exhibition and for the hell of it. Our ideas of enjoyment and exhibition have changed, and almost nobody drives for the hell of it any more.

The third major factor involved in the extinction of the ragtop was *business*. Making convertibles is a snap. Marketing them is something else. Anything can be built; not everything can be sold. This was the ragtop's problem. It was eminently popular—American drivers continued to adore the convert. But increasingly they preferred to let others take the trouble to buy and operate them. The bulk of auto ownership now rests in the suburbs, which favor inexpensive, invulnerable, dependable, all-purpose practical cars. In the 1960's, this was not a realistic description of the ragtop. Nor was there much incentive for automakers to try to change this prevailing trend. For years, the high-margin end of the auto business has been for options and the "after-market"—maintenance, repairs, parts and accessories. The real profits lie with the number of convenience/comfort/luxury items one can stack onto the basic automobile. Air conditioning, posh interior packages and stereo software were a major hunk of the auto industry's cash flow and were not particularly suited to an open car. If the convertible was not actually discouraged, it was at least marketed with a notable lack of enthusiasm and was hurt as much by corporate benign neglect as by anything else. While the convertible's decline was partly a lesson in sociology, it was also one of the more successful cases of planned obsolescence.

The difference between promoting an item and merely offering it is significant and accounts for the success of disposable razors and butane lighters, which would be minor novelties but for saturation PR. No idea is so outlandish or impractical that it can't be made rational by advertising. To the moguls of Big Auto who wanted to scrap the irresponsible, regulation-ridden, low-profit, low-accessory convert, its decreasing popularity was a blessing. This was no industrial conspiracy—just sound economics, which can be far deadlier. In business, to the unemotionally pragmatic go the spoils; and only the powerfully oblivious or possessed seriously proposed that the convertible be given special, endangered-species protection. As former GM president C.E. Wilson once told the Senate, "What's good for the country is good for GM, and what's good for GM is good for the country." Thus the demise of the open car was seen as not just necessary, but in everyone's best interests.

Even so, without the open car something was missing. The memory of the sun browning your body and the wind washing your face while you tooled through the boondocks trying to get one station at a time on the radio was more than mere nostalgia. It was Lost Fun. Few losses are more poignant or more difficult to make up for. God knows we've tried—churning out automotive fun-technology at a stirring rate, from car TVs and waterbeds to musical horns and sunroofs.

Indeed, the last ten years have seen a flood of styling, technological and model options designed to duplicate the ragtop as much as possible without actually building one. Vinyl tonneau roofs approximate the look of the cloth top while keeping out the bugs, cold and car thieves. Car stereo replaces the wail of the wind with the wail of music, and the CB radio puts us back within shouting distance of nearby vehicles; actual PA systems are now the rage. The sunroof admits fresh air and provides an outdoorsy touch without mangling one's new razor cut. Custom styling packages, options too numerous to count and visual accessories compensate for some of the ragtop's lost flare and allure. Vans with exteriors like Van Goghs and interiors like motel rooms express without revealing or inconveniencing. Air conditioning defrays the hothouse effect of summer.

All this may not represent a conscious attempt to duplicate the convertible with ersatz devices, but it's evident that a robust chunk of the auto industry consists of automotive technology designed to provide for a few dollars more what the ragtop once provided for nothing. Alas, it's just not the same. The tonneau roof is still a hard, immobile covering. CB radios are but lonely imitations of the direct communication between open car drivers. The sunroof is a lame approximation of no roof at all, and although the sentiment behind it is nice—and the markup even nicer—you'll get more actual sunlight by washing such a car than by driving it.

This have-your-convertible-and-beat-it-too urge is nothing new. The 1902 Cadillacs featured hard, detachable roofs. In 1915, Ford offered a $750 "coupelet"—a sedan in every way except for the top, which was retractable. The early T-Birds came with removable metal tops, and the Ford Skyliner, as earlier noted, went to the extreme of offering an actual hard top which raised and lowered like a soft one. These attempts were largely unsuccessful because they couldn't compete against the available alternative of the genuine article—the convertible.

Today it's a different story. Pseudo-convertibles and semi-open cars are now the only game in town and are rapidly proliferating in Detroit's attempt to satisfy a latent craving for top-down driving which will not die out. T-tops, Targa tops and moon roofs (clear plastic bubbles) are all elaborations on the basic sunroof concept, employed to maximize the convertible feeling. Hottest of these items is the T-top—basically a hardtop from the trunk to the front seatbacks, with a thin center overhead strip from there to the windshield and removable glass panels arching up the sides to the T-strip. Outfits that custom-make these for new hardtops are multiplying, and T-tops are a rapidly growing manufacturer's option, factory-available on half a dozen American cars. Ford is openly advertising "the Mustang T-roof convertible." Nevertheless, there's still a marked difference between taking off the entire roof and merely removing an overhead panel or two. Cars of the latter variety are more ventilated than actually open, and although they expose the driver to the sky above, the back seats shall never again see the light of day. There are also several companies which will simply hack the hardtop off select Buicks, Dodges, Chevys and Pontiacs and replace it with a custom-built top, and while this is becoming a strong market, it is only for those who can ante up the $10,000–$20,000 alteration price.

We'll know that the convertible is a precious commodity when you can support a whole car lot selling nothing but ragtops. Well, the future is now. Here is Dave Granados' "Gasoline Alley" in Lafayette, California. As of its opening in the spring of 1977, it was the only known dealership devoted almost exclusively to American converts. Since Dave is wearing a rut in the sidewalk between his office and the bank, it probably won't be the last. Today Lafayette; tomorrow . . .

[WE SAVED OUR HIDE, BUT TOTALLED OUR OUTLOOK]

LASTLY, THE MAIN FACTOR keeping American motorists so-near-yet-so-far from *bona fide* convertibles is *safety*. The Federal Government whipped itself into a virtual fury of consumer protection in the early 1970's, and Federal Motor Vehicle Safety Standard #208 in 1972 was one result. It laid down stiff passenger-safety requirements which utterly ignored such matters as design and model-type. This classically bureaucratic interference with consumer-choice didn't actually prohibit the ragtop, but it made production an economic impossibility, which was just as effective. The kicker was a requirement that a car's occupants be completely contained inside the car during a 30-mph rollover. A few automakers adopted Targa-top construction—a built-in roll bar and a totally removable panel over the front seats—which provided simple roof retraction without sacrificing structural integrity. The biggies like Chrysler and Ford elected instead to sacrifice convertibility and wage their battle against the code's proposed inflatable-airbag requirement, which would effectively solve the rollover problem (and most others) but would cost the industry a bundle to incorporate.

Interestingly, the convertible isn't illegal right now. Eleven months after rule #208 was enacted, the court threw it out, denying that the government had the authority to eliminate existing forms of personal transportation in the name of safety. Sports cars and convertibles were explicitly cited. People presumed to be legally competent to write checks were presumed equally competent to know and deal with the risks inherent in their purchases, argued the court, and the degree of protection a consumer requires is thus strictly his/her business. Unfortunately, by then the connie had been *de facto* outlawed for almost a year, and most automakers, who had seen rule #208 coming, had trimmed the convertible from their lines in 1971, and many simply terminated it in 1972. By the time the court's reversal came, the 1973 models had been out for three months, and only a handful were available with cloth roofs. Auto executives did not wring their hands over the departure of this low-revenue oddity, especially since its demise invigorated the market for all the pseudo-ragtop options mentioned above. Nor was this phase-out particularly publicized; the buying public, far from issuing an outcry, didn't even notice it until the last convert had rolled off the assembly line.

Any future ragtop resurgence is further hindered by the latest trends in the government crusade to protect us from damage at our own heedless hands.

Regulations have been proposed to require that every car sold in the U.S. be able to support $2\frac{1}{2}$ times its weight upside down. Such a law cuts two ways.

A retracting flip-top scheme from the Bertone design studios.

There are thousands of ways to see the Golden Gate Bridge, but this view is only available from one kind of car.

cuts two ways. While infringing on the open car's owner and driver, it does maximize consideration for the welfare of unwitting passengers. But it won't eliminate the ragtop from the roadway, or block the flow of new convertibles from Europe via Mexico and Canada to individual buyers, or diminish the car's desirability to thousands of persons unperturbed about dying on the highway. The law will only make the open car more expensive and difficult to own. As with most things prohibited for our own good, the convertible will merely grow more valuable and marketable.

For that matter, many of the convert's notorious hazards are more a matter of image than reality. The car is only singularly vulnerable in rollover situations, but these are a minute fraction of the lethal highway events which threaten our well-being. It takes a mighty collision or insane driving habits to roll a car, and your chances of surviving such an accident even in a hardtop are nothing to gamble on. With the emergence and proper use of seatbelts, much of the metal roof's extra effectiveness is minimized. Air-bags would reduce this advantage still further, and unit-welded support bars above the front and rear seats would provide most of the protection of a hard top. Let's also note that the center of gravity of the automobile has dropped a foot or so since the convert was in flower, and new cars, increasingly lighter and lower, are more unlikely to go belly-up, making this statistically a weaker threat than in the past. Cloth-top cars, with even less weight overhead, would be even less susceptible to rollover.

When it comes to the more common highway hazards—such as being blind-sided by a bus or pruned on the freeway by a crazed lane-changer—you're probably safer in an open compact car than in a Honda or Chevette. Convertibles had to pass windshield-pillar crush tests; head-on, rear-end and side-angle collision impact tests; and provide seatbelts. By law, they had to be as safe as sedans, as long as you kept them upright (which is not to deny the fact that rolling over or colliding at high speed in an open car is by and large worse for your health than doing so in a comparable sedan). But overall, the difference is not as great as it seems, and somehow we managed to live with those possibilities for 75 years. What changed with the dawn of the '70s was our attitude; there was no sudden realization that the ragtop was dangerous,

but rather the conclusion emerged that drivers were incapable of dealing with such hazards and must be legislatively shielded from them.

Another factor militating against the convertible was its top's slashability. Vandals were everywhere, we were told, lurking in wait for the opportunity to wreak mayhem on these fragile items. There is no ignoring this liability, but a straw-poll of several dozen ragtop owners indicates that almost none of them have actually suffered such abuse. There are also several defensive tactics available to reduce this threat: keeping one's car garaged when it's not in use is most effective; so is keeping the top down when it is. With regard to slashing-for-theft, one of the first rules of ragtopping is to leave the car unlocked, thus making such destruction unnecessary and implying that the owner is gone for just a moment and coming right back.

Slashing-for-sheer-destruction is largely a juvenile pastime and basically represents the act of mutilating that which the offender cannot him/herself own. But this begs the bedrock question. If ragtops were once again made widely available, the envy motive would be much reduced, and persons with cloth cars would be more inclined to respect them and far less eager to hack and trash, lest this trend catch on and induce them to be hacked and trashed in kind. Indeed, perhaps a nation of people in open cars, unable to risk rollovers, collisions or drunken spills, would exercise a sufficient degree of caution to avoid them as well. If people started viewing cars as fragile possessions, people would probably stop viewing and employing them as weapons, targets, or hostility-outlets. If everyone drove a convertible, the result might be not an increase, but a decrease in vandalism, death, suicidal idiocy and paranoia. There's always hope.

There's always technology, too. A return to the cloth top doesn't necessarily mean the *same* cloth. There are now waterproof, rip-proof, fireproof—even bulletproof—lightweight fabrics in existence which could provide as much protection against vandalism and theft as the average car window, and more than many locking mechanisms. Granted, such materials are in limited and costly supply right now, but if the demand and profit potential were great enough, Dow, Monsanto or Burlington could probably have an affordable super-strength top on the market by Christmas.

Phil Franklin's license plate declares his mint 1969 Camaro convert to be an "SF CAR." While it may not be as picturesque as the cable car, it is growing almost as rare, and now rides near the top of any Collectables list.

Lucky Frances Knight. Her Olds Cutlass convertible was made in 1972—the last year GM produced mid-size convertibles, and not long before these classically-designed, solid, luxurious, and powerful smaller cars evolved into the cranky, inefficient whales of later years. A GM convertible of this size, design and vintage is a better investment right now than the Krugerrand. And according to the owner, an attractive single American female, it is the best conversation-opener in human history.

So. GIVEN ALL of its mortal drawbacks, is the ragtop dead forever? A genuine answer to that requires a prophet, not a writer, but a sane man can make a sensible case for the possibility that not only could it resurge, but that there's a healthy argument in favor of its doing so.

"If automobile companies can't make any money making something, they'll quit making it," notes collector Charles C. Allen, contending that the convertible, being a specialty item, is through. But who's to say they *couldn't* turn a profit with the ragtop? Cadillac executives who terminated the cloth El Dorado on the basis of buyer-rejection after sales dropped to 7500 units were soon kicking themselves with rueful amazement when 14,000 ElDos simply flew out of the showrooms in 1976. That may be a freak statistic, unique to the last-of-the-line phenomenon. But it may also indicate a widespread and intense fondness for the open car—an understatement, given the used-convert market—and a sign that the public misunderstood the convertible's doomed-species status until the very end. Now that it's gone, we miss it, perhaps even enough to buy one if it should return.

Other things have changed as well. From 1967–77 there were far too many different and simpler ways for the average driver to combine status, comfort and kicks on the thoroughfares. Air conditioning, tonneau tops and impressive power plants were all affordable and nails in the ragtop's casket. But we now face an imminent future of grim economics and grueling conservation, and it's finally become clear that the consumer will have to pick up the tab for America's voracious consumption of energy. Therefore, one of the first cuts you can expect is in the production of vehicles which provide all the comforts of home. We'll be lucky if *home* can still provide them.

Heating is no problem, being a free side-effect of a running engine, but as the price of auto air-conditioning edges up into the $500–700 range—especially given the overall rise of new car prices into the $7000 neighborhood—a lot of car buyers may decide to give this convenience some second thoughts. The cheapest and most efficient alternative could very well be a car whose top is removable. Granted, there are other less drastic means of ventilation, but they're not as functional and not particularly cheaper in retooling and design. Four open windows and a sunroof at high speed come close, but nothing will as quickly air out a locked and boiling automobile in a parking lot. If the winter of 1977 was a sensational argument against the ragtop, the summer of any year is just as strong an argument for it. T-tops are expensive halfway solutions at best.

Speaking of economics, we can't forget mileage.

The pseudo-convertible boom has produced jubilation among outfits making and selling such almost-open-car devices as the Moon Roof here—a basic motorized retracting sunroof, but of tinted glass.

The Dodge Challenger was perhaps the Secretariat of the pony cars. It was indiscreetly luxurious and powerful for its size, but its low, flat ominous look—like a scowling Cougar—intimidated all but a handful of buyers. Thus it was made for only two years—this is the 1971—and it would probably be easier to buy a whooping crane than an open Challenger.

In case you thought ragtop-ownership branded one as a fanatic or hopeless nostalgic, forget it. The upper crust is discovering these gems. Former Undersecretary of the Navy Paul Fay was so taken with his 1963 Lincoln Continental 4-door convertible that he got a 1966 version for Mrs. Fay to go with it. Nothing built today can touch these cars for distinctive and trouble-free driving, they insist. You, too, can drive a cabinet member. Gilt by association.

A car with a fabric roof, even with roll-struts, would weigh significantly less than a conventional hardtop. The actual gas money saved might be a little thing, but if the bind gets tight enough little things will mean a lot.

Indeed, no one can really foresee what the total impact of energy conservation will be. Abandonment by the automobile of liquid hydrocarbon fuels would create not just a ripple effect, but a tidal wave of innovation and experimentation. Cleaner burning fuels might make wind-in-the-face driving palatable again, and disarraying velocities of 55 mph won't mean much if our functional speed limit is around 40. If high costs limit our joyriding, they will similarly make it more of an event, to be enjoyed to the limit. Insofar as all this would tend to thin out extraneous traffic, the open road would be genuinely *open* again. Roadside blight, already on the downswing, would be further diminished. And should gas-sucking luxury cars, muscle cars and vans be taxed $500–$1000 for their ego-virtues, the convert would become the most affordable vehicle of dash and display.

In this vein, the greatest drawback of our destined vehicle—the economy car—is its size. It's barely built to hold human beings adequately, and cargo space ranges from not-quite-enough to nil. Even hatchbacks are limited to moderate-sized and normally-shaped objects. For *real* room in a small car—base drum room, antique sideboard room, two Doberman pinschers room—you need some provision to travel with the top removed. This is the simplest and thriftiest resolution to the standoff between miniaturization and utility.

Regarding privacy, there's no reason why a convertible can't offer all the seclusion and concealment of any metaltop. The need for a sexual asylum from a punitive straightlaced society simply doesn't exist any longer, and even for those who would spend time naked in clothtop cars, modern insulation, sealing and heating should provide an atmosphere as snug as any comparable sedan's.

They say the ragtop will never return, but that's what they said about bellbottoms in 1950. Times and fashions change. Should conspicuous luxury become social anathema, the ragtop, combining recreational indulgence and aescetic self-denial, could be the very blend of enjoyment and economy tastemakers will be pressed to come up with. The day may well dawn when even the loftiest of us will shop at the Tower of Levis instead of Bergdorf's, descend from Haig & Haig to chablis, and trade our rolling comfort-cells for open-top cars. If we are rained on in winter and bug-splattered in spring, well, that's the price of sacrifice.

Probably the closest thing to a genuine mini-convertible is the Lancia Scorpione, which is also as expensive as it sounds. The entire roof is cloth, and can be folded back and snapped into place rather like early VW sunroofs. Unfortunately, the joy of lowering the Scorpione's roof is limited, since it has almost no roof to begin with, and the effect is more sunroof than true open car. It is as fast to operate as a windowshade, but not much bigger.

Like the Bermuda Triangle, nobody can explain the MoPar Curse—the inability of top-quality used Chrysler Corporation cars to come anywhere near in value to their Ford and GM counterparts. This 1967 Plymouth Barracuda convert is just one example of many beautiful and powerfully-engineered autos which disappeared into the oblivion of low sales. The silver lining of this cloud is that items like the late-'60s 'Cudas often sell for half the going rate of comparable Mustangs. The MoPar curse is the investor's blessing.

Kay Taylor's 1966 Buick Skylark is the kind of ragtop that makes collectors flunk saliva tests, but she could care less. Dedicated to public transit and clean air, she dislikes cars altogether, and keeps her convert only because, of all things, it's so practical. Try packing a rain forest like this into your Rabbit. It's also an outstanding car for bass fiddle players and grandfather clock dealers.

At Least Not With The Top Down.❳

I F THE CLOTHTOP can be made to provide all the security, economy, status and comfort of a hard-top, the only question left is the fundamental one: will it sell? Nobody knows the answer. No one has tried to sell the *bona fide* open car for years. We know that the marketing clout of Ford, GM, Nissan and VW have proven the ability to get the public to swallow almost anything, at least to the break-even point, and we know that auto advertising is a force to be reckoned with on the glacier level. If Big Auto ever pulled out all the stops and really tried to move the thing, miracles might happen. More unlikely resurrections have occurred, and history—that most fickle of phenomena—has a way of rejecting tomorrow what it favors today, and vice versa. Unfortunately, as we grow serious about our problems, we're inclined to dismiss frivolous solutions simply *because* they're frivolous. We dearly love the ragtop, but from afar—from the cheap seats of stern reality. It is far easier to assume it's gone forever than to frustrate ourselves further with empty hopes.

We probably *won't* see its like again, but then, most of us probably won't give a damn. The ragtop remains precious only as rolling art, as a design and attitude now consigned to nostalgia. And if it's a shame

that more people don't appreciate its artistic merit, well, there's a lot of artistic merit around these days clamoring for appreciation. So, you can mourn the passing of the American ragtop, but take heart in the fact that as of April 14, 1976, this marvelous confection stopped being a commodity and started becoming history. This is a big improvement for any thing of real value.

Thus the open car leaves salesroom floors for good and goes where it probably belonged all along—into the hands of those persons obsessed with and devoted to its adoration and preservation. This may ultimately be the most fitting and proper role for the American convertible anyway, and it's enough that people are sufficiently fanatic to keep tens of thousands of convertibles in running condition, as living relics of a past we're better off remembering fondly than actually returning to. The ragtop will never truly die until the flame of self-evocation and joyride-narcosis dies out in the last of us. And then it won't matter.

In the meanwhile, gaze and admire and recollect. And try to ignore such poignant questions as the Chicago *Tribune* posed in its eulogy to the open car: "What are homecoming queens going to ride in?"

"A flame went out
when old-style convertibles died.
But now I'm all lit up again."

F●RD

When America needs
a better idea,
Ford puts it on wheels.

THE
CONVERTIBLE
KICK IS BACK

Ford announces the
Mustang T-roof
convertible. New
excitement from the
sweet-handling
Mustang II. Tinted,
see-through T-roof
panels come off in
seconds, store in the
trunk, and let the sun

(or stars) shine in.
Another feature that
sets Mustang apart
from other sporty cars
in its class. Clear your
head . . . see your
Ford Dealer.

FORD MUSTANG II

FORD DIVISION

Getting Serious About Investment.⟧

Investment is by definition a game played with large sums on a speculative basis and not a subject to be taken lightly. Since space did not allow us to take it heavily, we have minimized attention to investment-class convertibles and emphasized ragtops in the used-transportation category. But eventually *all* open cars will be investment items. Even now, many readers, motivated by some of the profit-minded statistics mentioned herein, will want more information on the investment aspects of convertible buying and selling.

We don't believe this is the place for all that, particularly since there are plenty of other places where such information can be found in abundance. If you aspire to the collector's-item level, we suggest you consider the following publications:

Hemmings Motor News. Probably the most comprehensive publication on car-collecting, it bills itself as the "World's Largest Antique and Vintage Car Marketplace," and with justification: it boasts 143,000 paid subscribers (as of May 1977) and monthly issues running better than 2000 pages each. These pages are filled primarily with classified ads broken into such sections as Services, Employment, Supplies, Tools, Chrysler/Ford/GM Parts, Literature, Miscellaneous; For Sale and/or Wanted. There are also hundreds of display ads for cars, books, manuals, parts, auctions, shows, swap meets, restorers, services, tools and parts sources, flea markets, museums, specialty-car insurance; you name it. Everything from club membership applications to 1955 Willys horn-rings is here, and if there's a Bible in this game, *Hemmings* is it. Subscription rates and info can be had by writing to: HMN Subscriptions, Box 100, Bennington, Vermont 05201.

Cars & Parts. This is a somewhat smaller version of *Hemmings*, available either by copy at $1 per, or by subscription—$6 for 12 issues as of 1977. Listed, for sale, or wanted are cars, books, parts, antique items, auctions, restorers, body specialists, auto finders, flea markets, insurance, swap meets, car shows, tops, fabrics, accessories, custom fittings, novelties, hauling trailers, shipping services, and so forth. For one or more issues, write: *Cars & Parts*, P.O. Box 299, 114 E. Franklin Avenue, Sesser, Illinois 62884.

Old Cars. This is a tabloid newspaper of about 90 pages which comes out twice a month with a 50¢ cover price. There are articles and columns on every subject from garage fires and license-plate-futures to collectors' professional secrets. It's extremely up-to-date on auctions, listing several dozen worldwide each issue. This is literally a collectors' trade paper and goes deeply into the arcana of antique auto investment: hard news, old-car price guides, countless announcements, want ads, business opportunities, books and book reviews, interviews, tips, and every automotive item that can be bought or sold. It's available by subscription—$7.50 a year as of 1977—and has a paid circulation of 88,000. Write: *Old Cars*, Iola, Wisconsin 54945.

Vintage Auto Almanac. This is published annually by *Hemmings*, which bills it as "A Most Complete & Entertaining Directory to the Old Auto Hobby." It runs the gamut from articles on buying, transporting and restoring, to lists of clubs, service/parts sources, restoration/maintenance firms, rare parts dealers, vintage car dealers, salvage yards and museums. It includes addresses for every car-collecting enterprise from custom trim to photo calendars. It's a good source for interiors and tops, but should be considered only as a supplement to, not a substitute for, one of the periodicals above. If unavailable at your library or bookstore, write to: HMN, Box 945, Bennington, Vermont 05201.

Old Cars (Annual) *Car Club Roster and Information Booklet.* A must for the joiner, this concentrates on the club aspect of car collecting. Along with a complete list of automobile clubs broken down by location and specialty, it provides all the How-to information for anyone looking to start a club: sample rules, by-laws, constitution, and suggestions for organization; how to hold and announce shows and meets, how to exchange information and publicity, even tips on putting out newsletters. It's available for $2.00 plus shipping from: *Old Cars*, Iola, Wisconsin 54945.

Two more publications you may want to look at are *The Milestone Car* and *Automobile Quarterly*. Both come out every three months, and while they are more illustrative and affectionate than purely informational, they often have valuable articles on finding, assembling, restoring and appraising collector-cars. The former is published by the Milestone Car Society, P.O. Box 1166, Pacific Palisades, California 90272. The latter is available from Auto Quarterly, Inc., 515 Madison Avenue, New York, N.Y. 10022. Contact them for rates.

All of these should probably be inspected beforehand at your local library; as with the cars themselves, you should know what you're getting before you buy. You may also want to go back and pour over several years' worth of back issues for random tips and insights. In the May 1977 issue of *Old Cars*, for example, Tim Howley's "Somewhere West of Laramie" column discussed the adaptation of a Keough or IRA tax-cutting retirement plan to car investment.

Specialty auto clubs constitute the virtual grapevine of investment car collection. But, as noted in the Introduction, if there are any strictly convertible-oriented car clubs in America, it's news to us. The only outfits that come close are the Retractable Ford Club (1761 National Road, Dayton, Ohio 45414) and the Classic Thunderbird Club, International (48 Second Street, San Francisco, California 94105), which involve cars that are necessarily convertibles. Beyond that, you'll either have to start a ragtop club yourself, or settle for one of the clubs concerned with your *make* of car—Ford, Dodge, Olds, etc. These are listed in the annual publications noted above. By the time you read this book, there will hopefully be several open-car clubs in formative stages. If not, be the first on your block. . . .

A Sample Ragtop Resurrection.⟧

Since every used car's history, wear and parts requirements are different, there's really no such thing as a "typical convertible restoration." But here's a firsthand example which might serve as a workable starting reference point for the would-be ragtop renovator. It involves our photographer, George Hall, who spotted a certain 1968 Pontiac GTO convertible going absolutely *begging* on a used-car lot in Houston for $495.

The car's first asset was just being a GTO—a notoriously strong appreciation line. It was Pontiac's milestone mid-size muscle car, with a unique Coke-bottle shape and the industry's first ding-proof rubber front bumper. GTOs are considered excellent finds both from the standpoint of collectability and for everyday driving. Some were all-out sprint cars—nasty hotrods with four-speed sticks and multiple carburetors. But others—like this one—were more like lavish compacts, combining vast horsepower and automatic transmissions with power options, elegant interiors and air conditioning. Either way, the GTO was the quintessential late-'60s automobile—an option-laden small performance car; smooth, fast, and opulent. It is an Investor's Hall of Fame shoo-in.

Careful inspection of this particular Texas tornado, however, revealed the usual used-car contradictions. The body was almost perfect—no signs of major damage—but minor sheet-metal work on the fenders and under the front splash panel was needed. The original white paint, though faded, was intact and sound, and the car enjoyed that most precious advantage—no rust. Its black vinyl interior was of near-showroom appearance, and the carpeting was in good shape. The previous owner had clearly been

appearance-conscious—no minor consideration in auto investment. However, vandals had been at the top—probably while the car sat on the lot—and once top integrity has been violated, the smart buyer must think replacement, not simply repair.

Under the hood, the picture was rather more grim. To be explicit, the big 400-cubic-inch V-8 engine had had it. The valves were hanging up; the rings were history. The usually-reliable GTO Turbo-Hydra-matic trans suffered slight seal leakage but shifted nicely, and its fluid was free of the dreaded *scorched* odor. Belts, hoses and the battery were universally in replace-at-once shape.

Elsewhere, so were both tail pipes, which were riddled with holes. And one muffler was on the critical list. The shock absorbers were good and stiff—probably heavy-duty replacements—but the tires were of the low-rent variety and would have to go.

The interior of the car was gadget heaven. But,

miraculously, everything worked. The dash featured a tachometer and the optional gauges instead of simple indicator lights. Power steering/brakes/windows, four-way seats, disappearing headlights, tilt steering wheel, and factory air conditioning were all in fine order. The odometer was functional and, at 92,000 miles, apparently honest. The clock didn't work. What else is new?

The importance of a thorough pre-purchase scrutiny and detailed check-out is nicely illustrated here. The salesman knew little of this car's history—having taken it in trade—and George was not only spared tales of little old ladies and weekly excursions to church, but the car's value became strictly a matter of visible condition. Confronted with George's exhaustive list of shortcomings, he had little to fall back on but candor, and seemed relatively glad to see the car hobble off for $375 cash. An hour's worth of inspection which saves $120 is time wonderfully spent.

George's next problem was a common but frequently unanticipated one: a car in one locale (Houston) which must somehow be gotten home to a far different one (San Francisco). In this case, the friendly fates provided some acquaintances who were making that very trek by van, and they towed the GTO to his door for a gracious, and unrealistically low, $100 fee. The alternative to such a lucky break—or to healthy shipping costs—is having the car brought up to long-haul driving condition by unfamiliar mechanics on a one-shot no-recourse basis.

At this point, George made Wise Decision #1—he handed the car over to a series of professional experts for the actual restoration work.

The first experts were Ed Fong and "Tommy" Tom, owner of San Francisco's Valencia Auto Service, who pulled out the engine, transmission, and radiator. The engine brought good news and bad. The good news was that the block and pistons were solid. The bad news was that almost everything else—lifters, rings, timing chain/gear, main bearings and more—would have to be replaced. Then came Wise Decision #2: having this and all other necessary work *done*. The valves were also ground. And the big Rochester four-barrel carburetor was rebuilt with a standard kit.

After a specialist decreed that the transmission would perform indefinitely with occasional shots of fluid to offset the slight leakage, it went back in. The engine compartment was cleaned, painted black, and filled with a totally rebuilt V-8, an overhauled radiator, and a great host of new miscellany—plugs, ignition wires, belts, hoses, battery, distributor, regulator; "God knows what all," phews George. Everything was made hospital-tray clean.

To facilitate the all-important post-operation test-drive, everything was made even more hospital-corridor quiet by replacing the bad muffler and both tail pipes. This was done with stock Pontiac parts and hardware to avoid the occasional make-it-fit torching and welding common to quickshot chain muffler shops. The vital test-drive was extensive, meticulous and satisfying to all.

The next expert was Gerhard Butter, owner of Redwood Tire Center, who provided four new steel-radial "blems"—factory seconds of solid constitution but with minor visual flaws. They were mounted on flash factory mag wheels acquired from a local junkyard—a popular and price-boosting option. Front-end alignments are seldom a waste of money, and

after the radials were electronically balanced, that job was also done.

Although now mechanically gorgeous, Hall's "Goat"—as GTOs were known to connoisseurs—was still somewhat tacky to the eye. Enter our third expert: Jeff Dunn of Elegant Auto Body in San Francisco, who smoothed out minor dents and replaced the front splash panel like a plastic surgeon. After removing as much chrome and insigniae as possible for clean, unbroken paint coverage, the car was given a day-long sanding, heavily prepped, and baked with a ruby red acrylic enamel.

Finally, Otis Harris of American Auto Upholstery in Oakland laid on the icing—a new black vinyl top. The original hard-glass rear window was retained for visibility and resale value.

The result, in the words of our cameraman/owner: "A dream machine; unspeakably fast, tight, and beautiful—a fitting reincarnation." Since restoration, the car has covered 16,000 miles with oil and filter changes every 2000 miles, a tune-up after 10,000, and one brake-relining. Beyond that, G. Hall's GTO has cruised elegantly and trouble-free. Its only remaining drawback falls under the mixed-blessing heading:

with a car this sleek, the owner is afraid to let it out of his sight—"for fear of what the unthinking rabble might do to it."

And, lest we forget the nut of the issue, the financial bottom line looks like this:

Cash purchase, including sales tax:	$389
California registration and smog test:	42
Engine overhaul; parts and labor:	688
Exhaust system; parts and labor:	102
Used mag wheels:	60
Four "blem" radials (mounted and balanced); plus front-end alignment:	202
Body repair and repainting:	397
Vinyl top, with installation:	173
Brake reline; parts and labor:	87
Towing fee; Texas to California:	100

Total: $2240

In the final analysis, not too shabby for a car that is (1) virtually new inside and out; (2) worth $3000 as it sits (in May 1977) and rising; and (3) a simply smashing red exuberance, the likes of which are no longer made.

Need we say more?

HOW MUCH GOLD IS LEFT IN THEM THAR HILLS?⟧

THERE ISN'T NEARLY ENOUGH DATA to figure with any precision the number of American convertibles still on the road. Auto registration records are too vague, inconsistent and dated. Some registered ragtops are little more than debris; some unregistered "junkers" are only a few hundred bucks shy of running condition. And so on.

But a book about converts would be horribly remiss if it didn't at least make a stab at estimating how many of this noble breed still cruise on the highways, and we've done this using figures taken from the 1977 volume of *Motor Vehicle Facts & Figures*, published by the Auto Manufacturers' Association.

We began with the Total Sales for each year from 1961 to 1974. We divided this into the industry's esti-mated number of vehicles from each year still on the road in 1975. This produced a survival-percentage for cars 1–14 years old (e.g. 56 per cent of ten-year-old cars. ten per cent of 15-year-olds, etc.). Then the number of convertibles manufactured each year since 1962 was multiplied by the appropriate percentage as of 1977. The result was our reckoning of the number of 1963–74 ragtops still on the roads. This figure is 1,097,500, give or take a few thousand.

We assume virtually all American ragtops made in 1975 and 1976 are still in existence (though most are probably not for sale): about 32,000. In 1961 and 1962, a total of 738,000 convertibles were built. At a purely arbitrary seven per cent survival rate, that's another 51,660. Finally, *MVF&F* estimates that

2,260,000 pre-1961 cars were still going strong in 1975. Based on general manufacturing patterns, a vast quantity of these are probably open cars, particularly pre-1930's survivors. A more realistic guess as to available, affordable convertibles from this pool would be about five per cent. Add a final 113,000.

Here is the resulting overall picture of Surviving American Ragtops:

Pre-1961:	113,000
1961 & 1962:	51,660
1963–1974:	1,097,500
1975 & 1976:	32,000
Total:	1,294,160

Out of some 115,000,000 registered automobiles in America, 1.2 million is not a strong proportion, but it's 1.2 million better than nothing. Using the Federal Highway Administration's 1974 estimate of 125,000,000 licensed drivers, this breaks down almost exactly to one surviving ragtop per 100 legal motorists. On the one hand, this means that if you want to beat the competition, you'd better join the race right now. On the other hand, it means you're only a cloth-topped car away from being, literally, a one-in-100 item on the road: a ragtop driver.

(Note—Bear in mind that these statistics could be as misleading as a bookie's tax return. Readers who feel this is the case are invited to take these or any other raw statistics and apply whatever formulae and interpretations appeal to them, to come up with a different figure. Your informed guess is probably as good as ours.)

Where the Toys Are.]

For the same reasons why it is impossible to state the precise number of available convertibles, it is also impossible to state with any accuracy where their highest concentrations are. But—again using the 1977 *Motor Vehicles Facts & Figures* —we can tell you which localities have the most registered motor vehicles in general, and then list those in which we, personally, would go ragtop-hunting.

There are eight states containing 4,000,000 or more vehicles: California (11.4 million), New York (6.7), Pennsylvania (6.3), Ohio (6.2), Texas (6.1), Illinois (5.4), Florida (4.8), and Michigan (4.6). Since a hospitable climate is less wearing on convertibles *and* tends to attract them, we would concentrate on California, Texas and Florida, in that order, with Ohio and Illinois as less-choice alternatives. By all accounts, there are good proportions of solid, rust-free open cars tooling through the Sun Belt—Arizona, New Mexico and Oklahoma—but these states' combined auto registration barely tops 3,000,000, and you're going to have a lot of ground to cover.

Let's try to be more specific. Taking *MVF&F*'s figures on the 28 most auto-populated cities in America, we can pinpoint the best-odds locales on that list for open-car shopping.

1. Los Angeles / Long Beach
2. New York City
3. Chicago
4. Detroit
5. Philadelphia
6. San Francisco
7. Dallas / Fort Worth
8. Washington D.C. area
9. Nassau / Suffolk
10. Houston
11. Pittsburgh
12. St. Louis
13. Atlanta
14. Cleveland
15. Minneapolis / St. Paul
16. Baltimore
17. Anaheim / Santa Ana
18. Denver
19. Miami
20. San Diego
21. Seattle
22. Tampa / St. Petersburg
23. Riverside / San Bernardino
24. Cincinnati
25. Kansas City
26. Phoenix
27. San Jose
28. Portland

Considering factors such as weather, road conditions, ragtop-marketing and popularity, we can narrow this down to under a dozen prime locales:

1. Los Angeles / Long Beach
2. San Francisco (Bay Area)
3. Dallas / Ft. Worth / Houston
4. Anaheim / Santa Ana
5. San Diego
6. Miami
7. Riverside / San Bernardino
8. Tampa / St. Petersburg
9. Phoenix
10. San Jose

Our reasoning went like this—

Clearly, the L.A. area is the premiere game pre-serve for convertibles in America. It is also spitting distance from several other major car concentrations, and if you're really dedicated, there's a good chance you'll wind up here.

If you include Oakland and the East Bay with San Francisco, this area is probably far closer to L.A. in ragtop-density than its #6 overall ranking would indicate. Most of the cars shown in this book came from this neighborhood, and we can personally vouch for its abundance in open cars.

Dallas / Ft. Worth and Houston are both in convertible country, and as far as we can tell, it's probably a

toss-up between them. (We are also not about to provoke any arguments with Texans.)

Anaheim / Santa Ana, which is to say Orange County, may actually have more convertibles than the Texas metropolises, but random reports indicate that Southern California ragtop prices are notably higher than those in the Lonestar State. There are a ton of open cars here, though.

Unless you're in the market for topline Cadillac/ Lincoln elegance, rate San Diego ahead of Miami. The former's prices may even be competitive with Texas. The latter's may be somewhat higher.

Riverside / San Bernardino is one of the custom-rod capitals of the hemisphere, and while you'll find a huge number of open cars there—including a large core of collector's restorations—most of them will be

anything but original—many won't even be stock—and will have seen hard driving and dubious mechanics. Be careful.

San Jose probably has more available convertibles than Phoenix, but it's almost certain that Arizona prices will be among the lowest in warm-weather America, and collectors tell of fantastic finds in this vicinity. We give Phoenix the edge.

Beyond these grade-A locations, we would clump together as second-choice cities the following: Atlanta, Cincinnati, Kansas City, Portland, St. Louis and Seattle.

In all cases, remember the points made in the WHERE TO BUY section of this book, and concentrate not on the central city, but the outskirts. Happy hunting, and good luck..

The Lincoln Cosmopolitan Convertible. White side-wall tires and road lamps optional at extra cost.

If you want a fine car that is one in a million, not like a million others...then you may drive the great new 1949 Lincoln Cosmopolitan anywhere, in any company, safe in the assurance you are driving the most distinctive fine car on the road. Lincoln Division of Ford Motor Company.

Lincoln makes America's Most Distinctive Cars

Fig. 1

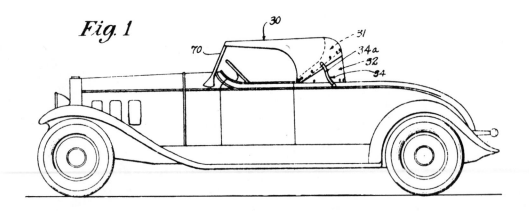

This book was set in Monotype Bembo
by Mackenzie-Harris Corp.
of San Francisco.
It was designed by Dugald Stermer
assisted by John Williams,
and edited by Leslie Timan.

Fig. 2

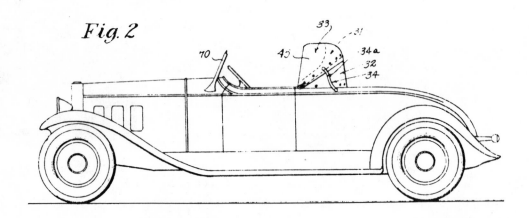

Fig. 3

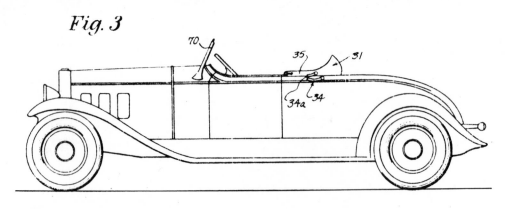